PIANO • VOCAL • GUITAR

MW01267563

Value Songbooks

1970s & 1980s HITS

PLAY THE HITS *for less!*

Produced by
Alfred Music Publishing Co., Inc.
P.O. Box 10003
Van Nuys, CA 91410-0003
alfred.com

Printed in USA.

ISBN-10: 0-7390-7115-7
ISBN-13: 978-0-7390-7115-1

CONTENTS

AFTERNOON DELIGHT

Words and Music by
BILL DANOFF

In a moderately slow country 2 ♩ = 76

F Bb/F

mf

F Bb/F

1. Gon-na

Verse 1:

F Gm7

find my ba-by, gon-na hold her tight, gon-na grab some af - ter-noon de-light. My

F Gm7

mot-to's al-ways been "When it's right, it's right." Why wait un-til the mid-dle of a cold dark night

C7
when ev - 'ry - thing's a lit - tle clear - er in the light of day,
Gm7
C7
and we know the night is al - ways gon - na be here an - y - way?
F
Gm7
Think - ing of you's work - ing up my ap - pe - tite, look - ing for - ward to a lit - tle af - ter -
F
noon de - light. Rub - bing sticks and stones to - geth - er make the sparks ig - nite and the

Chorus:
Gm7
F
thought of lov - in' you is get - ting so ex - cit - ing. Sky rock - ets in flight,
C
A7
Dm
af - ter - noon de - light,
Gm7
Am7
B♭
B♭/C
F
To Coda
af - ter - noon de - light,
Gm7
Am7
B♭
B♭/C
F
af - ter - noon de - light.
2. Start - ed

Verse 2:
F
Gm7
out this morn-ing feel-ing so po-lite, I al-ways thought a fish could not be caught who
did-n't bite. But you got some bait a-wait-ing and I think I might like nib-bl-ing a lit-tle af-ter-
D.S. 𝄋 al Coda
𝄌 Coda
Am7
B♭
B♭/C
noon de-light.
af - ter-noon de-light.
Guitar solo:

F
Gm7
Bridge:
Am7
B♭
Gm7
C
Be_____ waiting for me, ba-by, when I come a-round._____
Gm7
Am7
B♭
Gm7
C
We____ can make a lot of lov-ing 'fore the sun gone down._____
F
Gm7
Think-ing of you's work-ing up my ap-pe-tite, look-ing for-ward to a lit-tle af-ter-

F
noon de - light. Rub - bing sticks and stones to - geth - er make the sparks ig - nite and the
Gm7
thought of lov - in' you is get - ting so ex - cit - ing.
Chorus:
F
Sky rock - ets in
C
A7
Dm
flight,
af - ter - noon de - light,
Gm7
Am7
B♭
B♭/C
F
af - ter - noon de - light,

Gm7
Am7
B♭
B♭/C
F
af - ter - noon de - light.
Gm
3
Am
B♭
B♭/C
F
Af,
af - ter - noon de - light.
Gm7
N.C.
Af,
F
af - ter - noon de - light.

AT THIS MOMENT

Words and Music by
BILLY VERA

*Originally recorded in G♭ major.

1.
2.
Bridge:
C6
F
Am
B♭
F/A
Gm7
B♭/F
Dm
Am7
C/E
Dm7
love me__ no more?___
more?___
Did you think I___ could hate you or
raise my hands_ to you? Now come on, you know me too well.
How could I hurt you when, dar-lin', I love you? And you

Gm7
B♭/C
C6
know I'd nev - er hurt you, oh.
Verse 3:
F
Am/E
3. What do you think I would give at this mo-ment? If you'd
p
mf
Cm6/E♭
Dsus
D
Gm7
stay, I'd sub - tract twen - ty years from my life. I'd fall down on my
C6
Gm7
C6
Gm7
C13
knees, kiss the ground that you walk on, if I could just hold you a -

Saxophone solo:
F
Am/E
Cm6/E♭
gain.
Dsus
D
Em7(4)
D/F♯
Gm7
C6
I'd fall down on my knees, kiss the
Gm7
C6
Gm7
C13
ground that you walk on, ba - by, if I could just hold you, if
molto rit.
Freely
Gm7
C
I could just hold you, if

Gm7
C
I
could just hold
you
a - gain.
F
p a tempo
f
Am/E
Saxophone solo
B♭
C6
F
molto rit.

AGAINST ALL ODDS

(Take a Look at Me Now)

Words and Music by
PHIL COLLINS

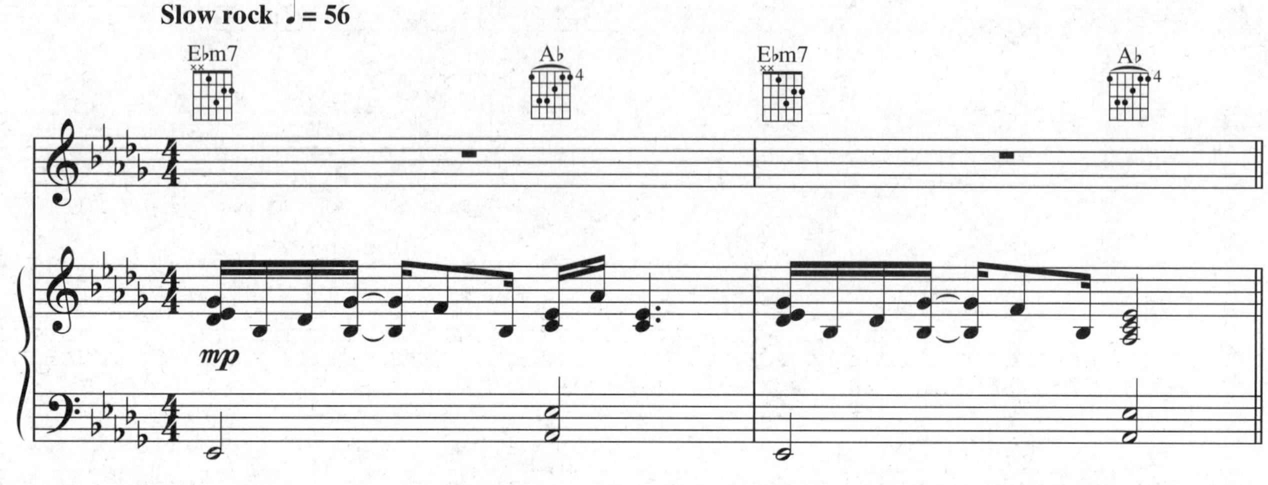

E♭m7 | 1. A♭

on - ly one who real - ly knew me at all.

2.3. A♭sus | A♭ | *Chorus 1 & 2:* D♭/A♭

So take a look at me now, well, there's just an

mf

E♭7/A♭ | B♭m | G♭

emp-ty space. And there's noth - ing left here to re - mind me, just the mem -

E♭m7 | A♭sus | D♭/A♭

'ry of your face. {Well, take a look at me now, / Now, take a look at me now,} {well, there's just an / 'cause there's just an}

E♭7/A♭
B♭m
G♭
emp-ty space. And you com-in' back to me is a - gainst the odds, and that's what
emp-ty space. But to wait for you is all I can do, and that's what
1.
E♭m7
A♭sus
A♭
D.S. 𝄋
I've got to face.
3. I
mp
2.
Chorus 3:
E♭m7
A♭sus
A♭
D♭/A♭
I've got - ta face. Take a good look at me now, 'cause I'll still be
f
E♭7/A♭
B♭m
G♭
stand-ing here. And you com-ing back to me is a - gainst all odds, it's the chance

Verse 2:
How can you just walk away from me,
When all I can do is watch you leave?
'Cause you shared the laughter and the pain,
And even shared the tears.
You're the only one who really knew me at all.
(To Chorus 1:)

Verse 3:
I wish I could just make you turn around,
Turn around and see me cry.
There's so much I need to say to you,
So many reasons why.
You're the only one who really knew me at all.
(To Chorus 2:)

ANGEL FROM MONTGOMERY

Words and Music by
JOHN PRINE

E A B E
this old house would-'ve burned down a long time a - go.
Chorus:
D A E
Make me an an - gel that flies from Mont-gom - 'ry, make me a post-
D A E D
er of an old ro - de - o. Just give me one thing that
To Coda
A E A
I can hold on to, to be - lieve in this liv - in' is just a

B E A E A
hard way_ to go.___
Verse 2:
E A E A
2. When I was a young girl,___ well, I___ had__ me a cow - boy.
E A B E
He weren't_much to look at, just a free ram - blin'_ man.___
A7 E A
But that_ was a long___ time,___ and no mat-ter how I try_

D.S. 𝄋 al Coda

E A B E

those years_ just flow_ by like a bro - ken - down_ dam.___

Coda

Bm7 G E A

hard_ way to go.

E A E A

dim.

Verse 3:

E A E A

3. There's flies_ in the kitch-en, I can hear 'em there buzz - in',

mp

E
A
B7
E
and I ain't done noth - in' since I woke up to - day.
A
E
A
How the hell can a per - son go to work in the morn - in'
E
A
B7
E
and come home in the eve - nin' and have nothing - ing to say?
cresc.
Chorus:
D
A
E
Make me an an - gel that flies from Mont - gom - 'ry,
mf

D
A
E
make me a post - er of an old ro - de - o.
D
A
E
Just give me one thing that I can hold on to,
A
Bm7
E
to be - lieve in this liv - in' is just a hard way to go.
A
B7
E
To be - lieve in this liv - in' is just a hard way to go.
molto rit.

ANNIE'S SONG

Words and Music by
JOHN DENVER

A7
G
rain.
Like a storm in the des -
A
Bm
G
D
D/C♯
ert,
like a sleep - y blue o - cean,
Bm7
D/A
G
F♯m
Em
you fill up my sens - es,
come
A7
D
Dsus
D
Dsus
fill me a - gain.
Come let me

G
A
Bm
G
love
you,
let me give my life
sens - es
like a night in a
D
D/C♯
Bm7
D/A
G
to you.
Let me drown in your laugh -
for - est,
like the moun - tains in spring -
F♯m
Em
G
A7
ter,
let me die in your arms.
time,
like a walk in the rain.
G
A
Bm
Let me lay down be - side you,
let me
Like a storm in the des - ert,
like a
(2nd time hold back...

G
D
D/C♯
Bm7
al - ways be with you.
sleep - y blue o - cean,
you
...a tempo)
D/A
G
F♯m
Em
A7
Come let me love you,
fill up my sens - es,
come love me a -
come fill me a -
1.
D
Dsus
D
Dsus
2.
D
gain.
You fill up my
gain.
Dsus
D
Dsus
D
Dsus
D

BABY COME BACK

Words and Music by
JOHN CROWLEY
and PETER BECKETT

Verse 1 (sing 1st time only):
A♭/B♭
Gm7
all my nights, all my mon - ey go-in' out on the town._
Verse 2 (sing 2nd time only):
2. All day long_ wear-in' a mask_ of false bra-va - do,_
A♭/B♭
Gm7
Do-in' an - y - thing just to get you off_ of my mind._ But when the
try'n' to keep up a smile_ that hides_ a tear._ But as the
A♭/B♭
Gm7
morn - ing comes, I'm right back where I start - ed a - gain._ And
sun goes down, I get that emp - ty feel - ing a - gain._

A♭/B♭
B♭/C
C
Cm7
try'n' to for - get__ you is just__ a waste__ of time.__
Ba - by, come back,
How I wish__ to God__ that you__ were here.__
Ba - by, come back,
𝄋 Chorus:
A♭maj9
Gm7
Cm
Fm7
Gm7
an - y kind of fool could__ see__ there was some-thing in ev - 'ry-thing__ a - bout__
Cm7
A♭maj9
__ you.
Ba - by, come back,
you can blame it
To Coda 𝄌
1.
Gm7
Cm
Fm7
Gm7
Cm
D♭maj9
all on__ me.__ I was wrong__ and I just__ can't live with-out__ you.

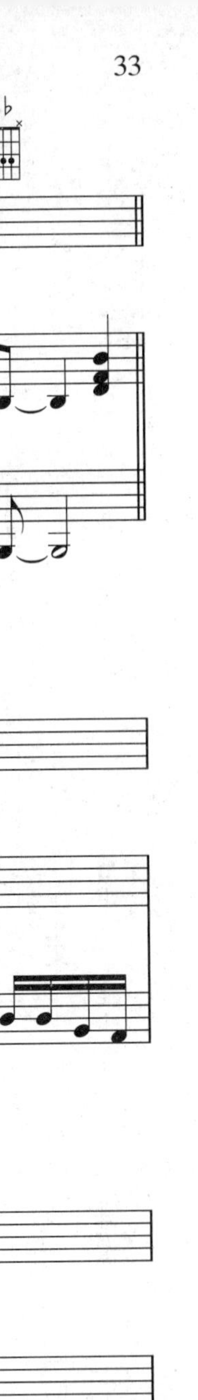

2.

A♭/B♭ Gm7 Cm D♭maj9 B♭sus B♭

you.

Bridge:

G♭maj7 D♭maj7

Now that I put it all to-geth-er,

G♭maj7 D♭maj7

give me the chance to make you see.

G♭maj7 Fm7 B♭m

Have you used up all the love in your heart?

D.S. 𝄋 al Coda
A♭/B♭
N.C.
Noth-in' left for me, ain't there noth-in' left for me?
Ba-by, come back,
Coda
Cm7
Fm7
Gm7
Cm
B♭/D
Cm7
you. I was wrong and I just can't live.
dim.
mp
f
Outro:
A♭maj9
Gm7
Cm7
Fm7
Gm7
Cm
B♭/D
Cm7
(Guitar solo ad lib.)
Repeat and fade
A♭maj7
Gm7
Cm7
Fm7
Gm7
Cm
B♭/D
Cm/E♭
Gm7

BAD COMPANY

Words and Music by
PAUL RODGERS and SIMON KIRKE

*Original recording in E♭ minor, Guitars tuned down 1/2 step.

Dsus D
Des - ti - ny, oo, is the ris - ing
Chose a gun and threw a - way the
(8vb)
Em D/E Em
sun. Oh, I was born
sword. Now these
(8vb)
Dsus D Em
six - gun in my hand. Be-hind a gun
towns, they all know our name. Six - gun
(8vb)

Dsus
D
Em
I'll make my fi - nal stand,
sound
is our claim to fame.
(8vb)
D/E
Em
E5
G5
3
hey.
It's why they call me...
I can hear them say...
(8vb)
D5
5
A5
5
E5
7
D5
5
Chorus 1 (sing 1st time only):
Bad com - pa - ny and I can't de - ny.
Chorus 2 (sing 2nd time only):
Bad com - pa - ny and I won't de - ny.
f

E5
G5
A5
Bad company till the day I
Bad, bad com - pa-ny till the day I
E5
D5
E5
D5
die.
Oh, till the day I die.
die. Hi, oh yeah. Till the day I die.
1.
E5
Em
Till the day I die.
8vb

2.
E5
Em
2. Reb - el
Oo.
Guitar solo ad lib.
D
Em
D
E5
D/E
E5
(end Gtr. solo)
G5

Chorus 3:

D5
A5
E5
D5
Bad company, I can't deny.
E5
G5
A5
Bad company till the day I
E5
D5
E5
D5
die.
E5
G
D5
A5
That's what I said. It's bad company, oh yeah,

E5
D5
E5
A5
yeah,
yeah.
Bad
com - pa - ny
G5
E5
D5
till the day
I
die.
E5
D5
E5
Repeat ad lib. and fade
D5
E5
D5
E5
(with vocal and Gtr. ad libs.)

CELEBRATION

Words and Music by
RONALD BELL, CLAYDES SMITH,
GEORGE BROWN, JAMES TAYLOR,
ROBERT MICKENS, EARL TOON,
DENNIS THOMAS, ROBERT BELL
and EUMIR DEODATO

Moderately ♩ = 116

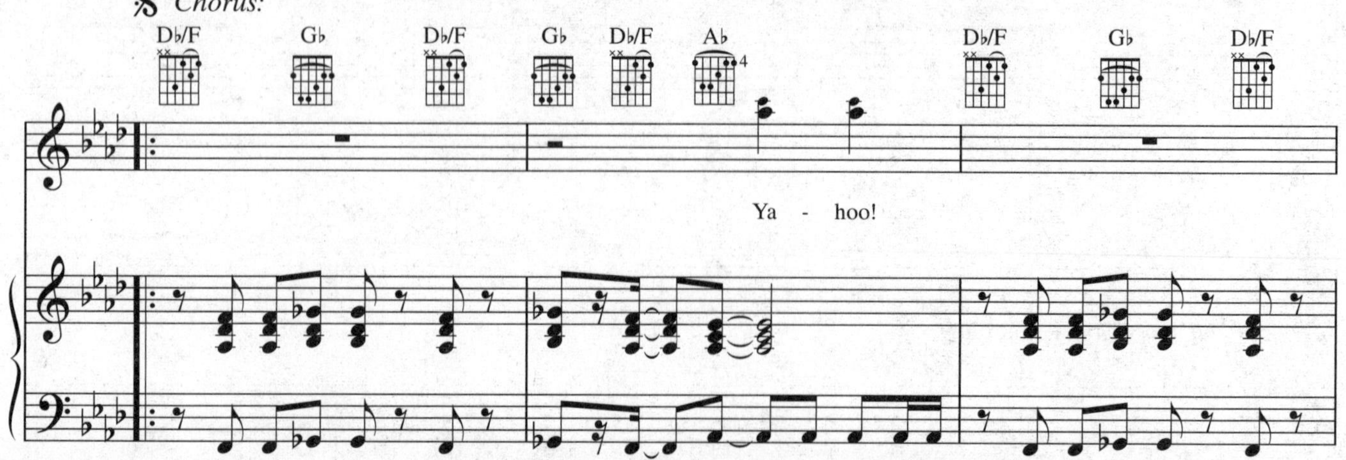

G♭
D♭/F
A♭
Week-end cel - e - bra - tion.
Ya - hoo!
It's a cel - e - bra - tion.
Cel - e - brate good times, come on!
Let's cel - e - brate.
To Coda
Cel - e - brate good times, come on!
Let's cel - e - brate.

Verse:
G♭
D♭/F
A♭
G♭/A♭
D♭/A♭
A♭
1.2. There's a party go-ing on right here, a cel-e-bra-tion / ded-i-ca-tion to last through-out the years.
So, bring your good times and your laugh-ter too.
We gon' cel-e-brate your / and party with you. Come on now.
(Cel-e-bra-tion.)
Let's all cel-e-brate and

D♭/A♭
A♭
G♭/A♭
D♭/A♭
A♭
have a good time.
(Cel - e - bra - tion.)
G♭/A♭
D♭/A♭
A♭
Bridge:
D♭maj9
We gon' cel - e - brate and have a good time.
It's time to
Cm7
Cm7/F
F
come to - geth - er.
It's up to you.
What's your plea - sure?
B♭m7
1.
B♭m7/E♭
2.
B♭m7/E♭
D.S. 𝄋 al Coda
Ev - 'ry - one a - round the world, come on!
round the world, come on!

Coda
Bridge:
Chorus:
Gb
Db/F
Ab
Gb/Ab
Db/Ab
We're gon-na have a good time to-night.
Let's cel-e-brate.
It's al-right.
Ba-by.
(Cel-e-bra-tion.)
Ya-hoo!

Db/F
Gb
Ab
4
Ya - hoo!
Cel - e - brate good times, come on!
(Vocal ad lib....
Let's cel - e - brate.
Cel - e -
Repeat ad lib. and fade
brate good times, come on!
It's a cel - e - bra - tion.

CAT'S IN THE CRADLE

Words and Music by
HARRY CHAPIN and SANDY CHAPIN

D A G G/F#
B♭ F E♭ E♭/D
He learned to walk while I was a - way. And he was talk - in' 'fore I knew it and
lot to do." He said, "That's o - kay." And he, he walked a - way, but his
shook his head and he said with a smile, "What I'd real - ly like, Dad, is to
Em7 Em/D C Em/B 1.2. A
Cm7 Cm/B♭ A♭ Cm/G F
as he grew, he'd say, "I'm gon - na be like you, Dad. You
smile nev - er dimmed. It said, "I'm gon - na be like him, yeah. You
bor - row the car keys. See you lat - er. Can I
C Em/B A
A♭ Cm/G F
To Next Strain
know I'm gon - na be like you."
know I'm gon - na be like him."
And the
cresc.
3. A
F
have them, please?"
And the
Chorus:
A
F
cat's in the cra - dle and the
cresc.
mf

G
C
D
E♭
A♭
B♭
sil - ver spoon,
Lit - tle Boy Blue and the man in the moon.
A
G
C
Em/B
F
E♭
A♭
Cm/G
1.2. "When you com - in' home, Dad?" "I don't know when, but we'll get to - geth - er then,
3. "When you com - in' home, Son?" "I don't know when, but we'll get to - geth - er then,
1.2.
A
C
Em/B
A
F
A♭
Cm/G
F
Son. You know we'll have a good time then."
Dad. You know we'll have a good time
A5
F5
mp

Em7
Cm7
A
F
D.S. 𝄋
3.
A
F
2. My
3. Well, he
then."
F
Db
G
Eb
Em
Cm
A
F
F
Db
G
Eb
Em
Cm
A
F
Verse 4:
A
F
4. I've long since re - tired, my

C
D
A
A♭
B♭
F
son's moved a - way. I called him up just the oth - er day.
C
A♭
I said, "I'd like to see you if you don't mind." He said, "I'd
D
A
B♭
F
love to, Dad, if I could find the time. You see, my
G
G/F#
Em7
Em/D
C
Em/B
E♭
E♭/D
Cm7
Cm/B♭
A♭
Cm/G
new job's a has - sle and the kids have the flu, but it's sure nice talk - in' to

A C Em/B A
F A♭ Cm/G F

you, Dad. It's been sure nice talk - in' to you."

G G/F♯ Em7 Em/D
E♭ E♭/D Cm7 Cm/B♭

And as I hung up the phone, it oc - curred to me, he'd

mp

C Em/B A C Em/B
A♭ Cm/G F A♭ Cm/G

grown up just like me. My boy was just like

Chorus:

A
F

me. And the cat's in the cra - dle and the

mf

G
C
D
E♭
A♭
B♭
sil - ver spoon,
Lit - tle Boy Blue and the man in the moon.
A
G
C
Em/B
F
E♭
A♭
Cm/G
"When you com - in' home, Son?" "I don't know when, but we'll get to - geth - er then,
A
C
Em/B
A
A5
F
A♭
Cm/G
F
F5
Dad. We're gon - na have a good time then."
rit.
a tempo
mp
Em7
A
Cm7
F
poco rit.

ESCAPE
(The Piña Colada Song)

Words and Music by
RUPERT HOLMES

C
Em7(♭5)
F
Fmaj7/A
G7
F
Dm/G
like a worn-out re-cord-ing of a fa-vor-ite song.
but me and my old la-dy have fall-en in-to the same
I knew her smile in an in-stant. I knew the curve of her face.
C
Cmaj7/E
Dm7
C
Em7(♭5)
F
Fmaj7/A
G7
old dull rou-tine.
So while she lay there sleep-ing,
So I wrote to the pa-per,
It was my own love-ly la-dy,
F
Dm/G
C
Cmaj7/E
Dm7
C
Em7(♭5)
I read the pa-per in bed,
took out a per-son-al ad.
and she said, "Oh, it's you."
and in the per-son-al col-
And though I'm no-bod-y's po-
Then we laughed for a mo-

F Fmaj7/A G7 F Dm/G C Cmaj7/E Dm7
umns there was this let - ter I read:
et, I thought it was - n't half bad:
ment, and I said, "I nev - er knew
Chorus:
C Em7(♭5) F Fmaj7/A G7 F Dm/G
"If you like pi - ña co - la - das and get - ting caught in the
"Yes, I like pi - ña co - la - das and get - ting caught in the
that you like pi - ña co - la - das, get - ting caught in the
C Cmaj7/E Dm7 C Em7(♭5) F Fmaj7/A G7
rain, if you're not in - to yo - ga,
rain. I'm not much in - to health food;
rain, and the feel of the o - cean

F
Dm/G
C
Cmaj7/E
Dm7
C
Em7(♭5)
if you have half a brain,
I am in - to cham - pagne.
and the taste of cham - pagne.
if you like mak - ing love at
I've got to meet you by to -
If you'd like mak - ing love at
F
Fmaj7/A
G7
F
Dm/G
C
Cmaj7/E
Dm7
mid - night
mor - row noon
mid - night
in the dunes on the Cape,
and cut through all this red tape,
in the dunes on the Cape,
C
Em7(♭5)
F
Fmaj7/A
G7
F
Dm/G
then I'm the love that you've looked for.
at a bar called O' - Mal - ley's
you're the la - dy I've looked for.
Write to me and es -
where we'll plan our es -
Come with me and es -

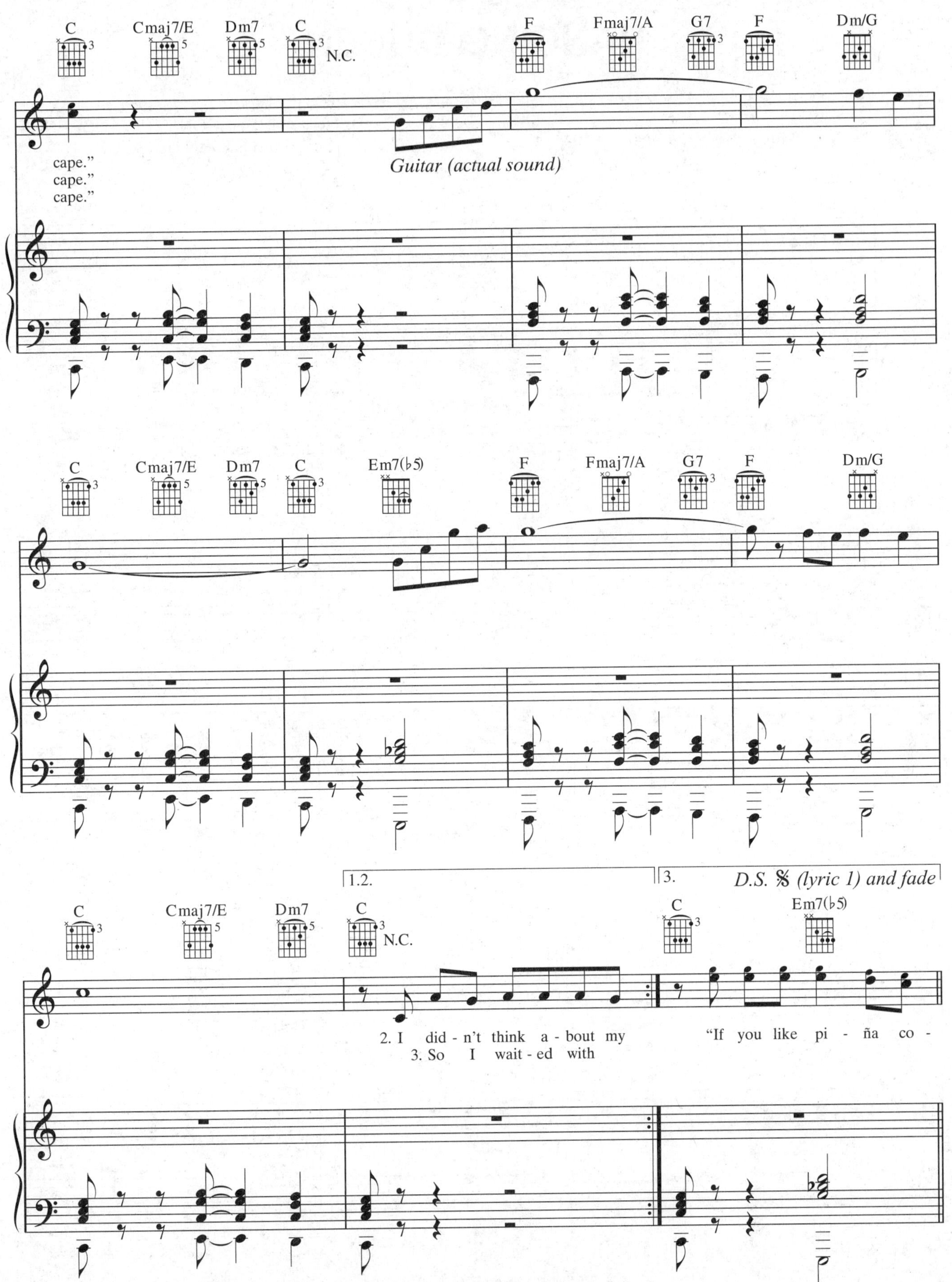
C
Cmaj7/E
Dm7
C
N.C.
F
Fmaj7/A
G7
F
Dm/G
cape."
cape."
cape."
Guitar (actual sound)
C
Cmaj7/E
Dm7
C
Em7(♭5)
F
Fmaj7/A
G7
F
Dm/G
1.2.
3.
D.S. 𝄋 (lyric 1) and fade
C
Cmaj7/E
Dm7
C
N.C.
C
Em7(♭5)
2. I did - n't think a - bout my
3. So I wait - ed with
"If you like pi - ña co -

DANCING QUEEN

Words and Music by
BENNY ANDERSSON, STIG ANDERSON
and BJORN ULVAEUS

E
C#7
F#m
You can dance, you can jive, hav - ing the time of your
B7/D#
D
Bm7
E7
life, ooh. See that girl, watch that scene, dig-gin' the
A
D/A
A
D/A
danc - ing queen.
Verse 1:
A
D/A
A
D/A
1. Fri - day night and the lights are low,

A
F♯m
look - ing out for a place to go, oh,
E
A/E
E
A/E
where they play the right mu - sic, get - ting in the swing, you've come to
E
F♯m
E
F♯m
look for a king.
Verses 2 & 3:
A
D/A
2. An - y - bod - y could be that guy;
3. You're a teas - er, you turn 'em on;

A
F♯m
night is young and the mu-sic's high.
leave 'em burn - ing and then you're gone.
E
A/E
E
A/E
With a bit of rock mu-sic, ev-'ry-thing is fine;
Look-ing out for an-oth-er, an-y-one will do;
you're in the
E F♯m
E F♯m
Bm7
mood for a dance.
And when you get the chance,
Chorus:
E7
A
D/A
you are the danc-ing queen,
young and sweet, on - ly

A
D/A
A
sev - en - teen.
Danc - ing queen,
D/A
A
E/G♯
D/F♯
A/E
feel the beat from the tam - bou - rine, oh yeah.
E
C♯7
F♯m
You can dance, you can jive, hav - ing the time of your
B7/D♯
D
Bm7
E7
life, ooh. See that girl, watch that scene, dig-gin' the

A
D/A
danc - ing queen.
1.
2.
Dig-gin' the
Repeat and fade
Oh,
oh.

DESPERADO

Words and Music by
DON HENLEY and GLENN FREY
Slowly ♩ = 72
G
G7
C
Cm6
mf
(with pedal)
G
Em
A7
D
Des - per - a -
G
G7
C
Cm6
do, why don't you come to your sens - es? You been
mp a tempo
G
Em
A7
D7
out rid - in' fenc - es for so long now. Oh, you're a

G
G7
C
Cm6
hard one, I know that you got your rea - sons, these
G/D
G+/D♯
Em
A7
D7
G
D/F♯
things that are pleas - in' you can hurt you some - how. Don't you
cresc.
Em
Bm7
C
G
draw the queen of dia - monds, boy, she'll beat you if she's a - ble. You know the
mf
Em
C
G
D/F♯
queen of hearts is al - ways your best bet. Now it

Em7
Bm7
C
G
seems to me some fine things have been laid up-on your ta-ble, but you
Em
A7
Am7/D
D
on-ly want the ones that you can't get. Des-per-a-
poco rit. decresc.
G
G7
C
G/B
Am7
do, oh, you ain't get-tin' no young-er, your
a tempo
G
D/F♯
Em
A7
D7
pain and your hun-ger, they're driv-in' you home. And

G
G7
C
G/B
Am7
free-dom, oh, free-dom, well, that's just some peo-ple talk - in'. Your
G/D
G+/D♯
Em
A7
D7
G
D/F♯
pris-on is walk-in' through this world all a - lone. Don't your
cresc.
Em
Bm7
C
G
feet get cold in the win-ter-time? The sky won't snow and the sun won't shine. It's
mf
Em
C
G
D
hard to tell the night-time from the day. You're

Em7
Bm7
C
G
los - in' all your highs and lows. Ain't it fun - ny how the feel - ing goes
Am7
C/D
D
G
G7
a - way? Des - per - a - do, why don't you
C
Cm6
G
D/F♯
Em
come to your sens - es? Come down from your fenc - es,
3
A7
D7
G
G7
3
o - pen the gate. It may be rain - in', but there's a

C
C6
G
D/F♯
Em
rain-bow a - bove_ you. You bet - ter let some - bod - y love you,
C
G/B
Am7
Am7/D
G/D
G+/D♯
Em
you___ bet - ter let some - bod - y love___ you_________ be -
Am7/D
G
G7
fore it's too_________________ late.
mp
a tempo
C
Cm6
G(9)
rit.

DON'T STOP BELIEVIN'

Words and Music by
JONATHAN CAIN, NEAL SCHON
and STEVE PERRY

A
E
B
lone - ly world. She took the mid-night train go - ing
South De - troit. He took the mid-night train go - in'
cheap per - fume. For a smile they can share the night, it goes
wants a thrill, pay - in' an - y - thing to roll the dice just
sing the blues. Oh, the mov - ie nev - er ends, it goes
1. 4.
G♯m
A
2.
G♯m
A
D.C.
an - y - where.
one more time.
an - y - where.
3. 5.
G♯m
A
B/A
A
on and on and on and on.
Strang - ers
Street - light
cresc.
f

B/A
A
B/E
E
B/E
E
wait - ing, up and down the bou - le - vard, their
peo - ple, liv - ing just to find e - mo - tion,
1.3.
B/A
A
B/A
A
B/E
E
shad - ows search - ing in the night.
hid - ing
2.4.
B/E
E
B/A
A
B
E
B
E
A
To Coda
some - where in the night.
E
B
C♯m7
A
D.S. al Coda

Coda
E
B
C♯m
A
(Inst. solo ad lib....
E
B
G♯m
A
E
B
C♯m7
A
Don't_ stop_ be - liev - in',_ hold on to the feel - in'._
Repeat ad lib. and fade
E
B
G♯m
A
Street - light_ peo - ple._

DON'T STOP 'TIL YOU GET ENOUGH

Written and Composed by
MICHAEL JACKSON

B
Verse:
B
A/B
B
1.Love - ly
is the feel - ing now.
2.Touch me
and I feel on fire.
A/B
Fe - ver,
tem-p'ra-tures
Ain't noth - ing
like a
B
ris - in' now.
love de - sire.
I'm

B
A/B
B
Pow - er
is the force, the vow
melt - ing
like hot can - dle - wax.
3. Heart - break,
en - e - my des - pise.
A/B
that makes it hap - pen,
and there's no
Sen - sa - tion
love - ly
E - ter - nal
love shines
B
A/B
ques - tions why.
Oo, get clo - ser
where we're at.
Oo, so let love
in my eyes.
Oo, so let love

B
to my bod - y___ now,___ so
take us through the___ hours.___ I won't be com-
take us through the___ hours.___ I won't be com-
A/B
B
love me,___ 'til you don't know how.___
plain - ing,___ this is love pow - er.___
plain - ing.___ Your love is all mine.___
Chorus:
Amaj7/B
___ Oo.___ Keep on___ with the force, don't stop. Don't stop 'til you get e-nough._ Keep on_
___ Oo.___
___ Oo.___
B
___ with the force, don't stop. Don't stop 'til you get e - nough._ Keep on_

Amaj7/B
with the force, don't stop. Don't stop 'til you get e - nough. Keep on
B
To Coda
1.
N.C.
with the force, don't stop. Don't stop 'til you get e - nough.
2.
N.C.
Don't stop 'til you get e - nough.
B
Bm7/E
E/F♯
G♯m7
A
B
Bm7/E
E/F♯
1.
G♯m7
A
B

2.
G♯m7
B
A/B
(strings)
B
A/B
B
D.S. 𝄋 al Coda

Coda
Verse:
B
A/B
Don't stop 'til you get e - nough._ 4. Love - ly_ is the
B
A/B
feel - ing_ now._ I won't_ be com-plain - ing,_
B
the force is love pow - er._ Oo._ Keep on_

Amaj7/B
with the force, don't stop.
Don't stop 'til you get e - nough. Keep on
B
with the force, don't stop.
Don't stop 'til you get e - nough. Keep on
Amaj7/B
with the force, don't stop.
Don't stop 'til you get e - nough. Keep on
B
Repeat ad lib. and fade
with the force, don't stop.
Don't stop 'til you get e - nough. Keep on

THE END OF THE INNOCENCE

Words and Music by
DON HENLEY and B.R. HORNSBY

B♭(9) Gm11 Gm7/C Gm11 F

moth-er and dad-dy stand-ing by.___ But "Hap-pi-ly ev - er___
tired old man that's no lon-ger king.___ Arm - chaired war - riors___
same___ small town in each of us.___ I need to re -

B♭(9)

af - ter"___ fails. We've been poi - soned by___ these___ fair - y tales.___ The
of - ten___ fail. We've been poi - soned by___ these___ fair - y tales.___ The
mem - ber___ this, so, ba - by, give___ me___ just one kiss.___ And

F Fsus F Dm7 B♭ *To Coda* 𝄌

law - yers dwell___ on___ small de - tails since dad - dy had___ to fly.___
law - yers clean up all___ the de - tails since dad - dy had___ to lie.___
come and take___ a___ long last___ look be - fore we say___ good -

C Dm7 F/A Gm11 B♭(9)

___ Oh,___ but I know a place where we can go that's
___ Oh,___ but I know a place where we can go and

Dm7
B♭(9)
C
Dm7
F/A
still un - touched_ by men.
wash a - way_ this sin.
Oh,_ we could sit and watch the
Gm11
B♭(9)
Dm7
B♭(9)
Csus
clouds roll by_ and the tall grass wave in the wind.
Oh, you can
Chorus:
F
C/F
B♭/F
C/F
Dm7
F/A
lay your head_ back_ on the ground_ and let your hair_ fall
Gm11
B♭(9)
F
C/F
B♭/F
F
all a - round_ me.
Of - fer up_ your_ best de - fense, but

Dm7
F/A
Gm11
B♭(9)
F/B♭
this is the end,
this is the end,
F/C
C7sus
F
F2
F
F2
Gm7
end
of the in - no - cence.
F/G
Am7/D
Gm7/C
B♭2
B♭(9)
1.
2. O
2.
Gm11
F/G
Gm7
Dm7
C
(Inst. solo ad lib.…

1.2.
3.
B♭
F/A
B♭2
F5
Fsus
F
B♭/F
C/F
B♭6/9/F
D.S. 𝄋 al Coda
Coda
C5
Gm11
bye.
You can lay
Chorus:
Dm7
Am
your head back on the ground and let your hair fall

Gm11 B♭(9) F Fsus F B♭/F

all a - round._ Of - fer up___ your___ best de - fense, but

Dm7 F/A Gm11 Dm7 F/A

this is the end, oh, this is the

Gm11 B♭2 Dm Gm11

end___ of the in - no-cence.

Repeat as desired for solos

Gm11 F/G Gm7 Dm C B♭

(Inst. solo ad lib....

Last time
B♭
F/A
B♭
F
Fsus
Chorus:
F
Fsus
F
Fsus
You can lay your head back on the ground,
F
Fsus
F
let your hair fall all a - round.
Of - fer up your
B♭/F
F
Dm7
F/A
Gm11
best de - fense. Oh, this is the end,
oh.

B♭
Dm7
F/A
Gm11
1.2.
1. This is the end
2. 3. ad lib. vocal melody
3.
F
F2
F
F2
Gm7
F/G
Am7/D
of the in - no-cence.
1.2.
Gm7/C
B♭
3.
Gm7/C
F/B♭
B♭
F
B♭
F
B♭
F
B♭
Csus
F
rit.

ENDLESS LOVE

Words and Music by
LIONEL RICHIE

E♭
E♭/F
Fsus
F
you're ev - 'ry breath that I take, you're ev - 'ry
I'll hold you close in my arms, I can't re -
B♭
F/A
E♭
step I make. And I,
sist your charms. And, love,
mf
E♭/F
F
B♭
F/A
Gm
Dm/F
I want to share all my love
I'll be a fool for you I'm
E♭
E♭/F
F
B♭
with you, no one else will do.
sure; you know I don't mind.

B♭9
E♭
E♭/F
F
And your eyes,
'Cause you,
they tell me how
you mean the
B♭
F/A
Gm
F6
E♭
much you care.
world to me.
Oh, yes, you will
Oh, I know
Dm7
Cm7
E♭/F
al - ways be
I've found you,
my end - less
my end - less
8va
1.
B♭
love.
mp

2.

B♭ E♭ E♭/F Fsus F

love.

mp

B♭

Bum, bum,

E♭ E♭/F

bum, bum, bum, bum, bum, bum, bum, bum,

B♭ E♭

bum, bum, bum. Oh, and, love,

cresc. *mf*

E♭/F
F
B♭
F/A
Gm7
F/A
3
I'll be that fool for you I'm
sure;
you know I don't mind.
E♭
E♭/F
F
B♭
B♭9
E♭
E♭/F
F
And yes,
you'll be the
on - ly one.
No one can de - ny
B♭
F/A
Gm
Dm/F
E♭maj7

Dm7
E♭maj7
Dm7
this love I have in - side. I'll
E♭maj7
Dm7
Cm7
give it all to you, my love, my love,
E♭/F
B♭
my end - less love.
p
E♭
E♭/F
Fsus
B♭
E♭/B♭
B♭
rit.

EVERGREEN
(Love Theme from *A Star Is Born*)

Words by
PAUL WILLIAMS

Music by
BARBRA STREISAND

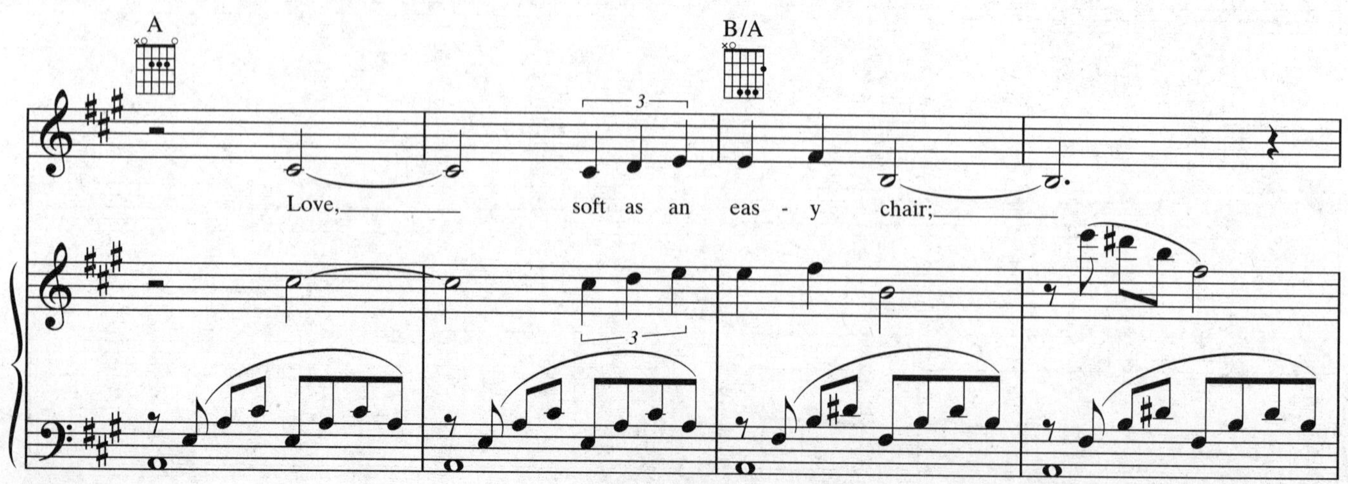

Bm/A
A
A/G♯
love, fresh as the morn - ing air.
F♯m
C♯m7
One love that is shared by two,
Bm7
G
I have found with you.
E
E7sus
E7
A
D/E
Like a rose un - der the A - pril snow,

Bm7
D/E
I was al - ways cer - tain
A
A/G#
F#m
love would grow.
Love,
age - less and ev - er - green,
C#m7
Dmaj7
Cmaj7
G/A
A7
sel - dom seen by two.
cresc.

Dmaj7
D6
C#m7
You and I will make each night a first,
E/D
G/A
A7
ev - 'ry day a be - gin - ning.
8va
G#7sus
G#7
C
Spir - its rise and their dance is un - re - hearsed.
A/B
B7
D/E
They warm and ex - cite_ us 'cause we have the bright - est
cresc. e allarg.

Amaj7
Gmaj7/A
love, two lights that shine as
Bm7
D/E
one, morn - ing glo - ry and the
A
A/G♯
F♯m
mid-night sun. Time, we've learned to
C♯m7
G/A
sail a - bove; time won't change the

Dmaj7 Dm(maj7) A

meaning of one love, ageless and

B/A B♭/A

ever ever

A B♭/A B/A C/A

green.

B/A B♭/A A

rit. e dim.

mp

EYE OF THE TIGER

Words and Music by
FRANKIE SULLIVAN III and JIM PETERIK

E♭/G
A♭
Cm
B♭/C
Cm
B♭/C
Cm
E♭/G
A♭
Cm
Verse 1:
Cm9
A♭/C
B♭/C
1. Ris - in' up,
back on the street;
did my time,
took my
sim.
Cm
A♭/C
chanc - es.
Went the dis - tance; now I'm back on my feet,
just a man

Verse 2:
B♭/C
Cm9
A♭
and his will to sur-vive.
2. So man-y times it hap-pens too fast.
B♭
Cm
You trade your pas-sion for glo - ry.
Don't lose your grip on the
A♭
B♭
Cm
B♭
Cm7
dreams of the past. You must fight just to keep them a - live.
It's the
Chorus:
Fm7
E♭/G
B♭
Cm7
Fm7
eye of the ti - ger; it's the thrill of the fight, ris - in' up to the chal-lenge of our

Cm7
B♭
Cm7
Fm7
E♭/G
B♭
ri - val. And_ the last known sur - vi - vor stalks his prey in the night, and_ he's
Fm7
E♭/G
A♭
N.C.
Cm
watch - in' us all with the eye of_ the ti - ger.
Verses 3 & 4:
A♭/C
B♭/C
3. Face to face,_ out in the heat;_ hang - in' tough,_ stay - in'
4. Ris - in' up,_ straight to the top._ Had the guts;_ got the
Cm
A♭/C
hun - gry. They stack the odds;_ still we take to the street for the kill_
glo - ry. Went the dis - tance, now I'm not gon - na stop; just a man_

Chorus:
B♭/C
Cm
B♭
Cm7
Fm7
with the skill to sur-vive.
and his will to sur-vive.
It's the eye of the ti - ger; it's the
E♭/G
thrill of the fight, ris - in' up to the chal-lenge of our ri - val. And the
last known sur-vi - vor stalks his prey in the night, and he's watch-in' us all with the
1.
A♭
N.C.
eye of the ti - ger.

2.
A♭
eye
N.C.
Cm
of the ti - ger.
B♭/C
Cm
E♭/G
A♭
The eye of the ti -
sim.
Repeat and fade
ger.
The eye of the ti -
sim.

GLORY OF LOVE

(Theme from *The Karate Kid Part II*)

Words and Music by
DAVID FOSTER, PETER CETERA
and DIANE NINI

C
F/A
B♭
E♭/G
I will al-ways love you,
I will nev-er leave you a-lone.
A♭
B♭/A♭
A♭
B♭/A♭
Verses 2 & 3:
C
G5
2. Some-times I just for-get,
say things I might re-gret,
3. You keep me stand-ing tall,
you help me through it all,
C
F5
C/G
G
it breaks my heart to see you cry-ing.
I'm al-ways strong when you're be-side me.

C/E
F/A
B♭/D
E♭/G
I don't want to lose you,
I could nev - er make it a - lone.
I have al - ways need - ed you,
I could nev - er make it a - lone.
A♭
B♭/A♭
A♭
B♭/A♭
Chorus:
C
F
C/E
G7sus
G
I am a man who would fight for your hon - or.
C
F/A
Dm9
G7
I'll be the he - ro you're dream - ing of.

Am7
Dm7
C/E
E/G♯
We'll live for - ev - er, know - ing to - geth - er that we
Am7
Dm9
G7sus
G7
1.
C
F/A
did it all for the glo - ry of love.
B♭
2.
C
F/C
C
Bridge:
Fm
A♭
B♭/D
B♭
E♭
Just like a knight in shin - ing ar - mor, from a long time a - go,

Fm
Ab
Cm7
Eb
Fm7
Bb
Eb
just in time I will save the day,
take you to my cas - tle far a - way.
Bb/D
F7sus
F7
Bb
Eb/G
Cm
Ab
Chorus:
Db
Gb
Db/F
Ab7sus
Ab
I am the man who will fight for your hon - or.
Db
Bbm
Ebm9
Ab7sus
I'll be the he - ro you've been dream - ing of. We're

Bbm7
Ebm7
Db/F
F/A
gon - na live for - ev - er, know - ing to - geth - er that we
Bbm7
Ebm7
Ab7sus
Ab7
Db
Gb
did it all for the glo - ry of love.
Db/F
Absus
Ab
Db
Bbm7
Ebm7
Ab7sus
Ab7
Bbm7
Ebm7
Db/F
F/A
We'll live for - ev - er, know - ing to - geth - er that we

B♭m7
E♭m7
A♭7sus
A♭7
did it all for the glo - ry of love.
B♭m7
G♭
A♭
We did it all for love.
B♭m7
G♭
A♭
We did it all for love.
Repeat ad lib. and fade
B♭m7
G♭
A♭
We did it all for love.

GREASE

Words and Music by
BARRY GIBB

Em7
D
C
Bm
E
Bm
There ain't no dan - ger we can go too far.
We start be - liev - in' now that we can
F#m7
G
be who we are.
Grease is the word.
Verses 2, 3, & 4:
Bm
E
Bm
E
Bm
2. They think our love is just a grow - in' pain.
Why don't they un - der - stand?
It's just a
3.4. We take the pres - sure and we throw a - way.
Con - ven - tion - al - i - ty
be - longs to
F#m7
Em7
D
C
Bm
cry - in' shame.
Their lips are ly - ing, on - ly real is real.
We stop the
yes - ter - day.
There is a chance that we can make it so far.
We start be -

Chorus:
E
Bm
F♯m7
Bm
fight right now. We got to be what we feel.
liev - ing now that we can be who we are.
Grease is the word.
Em7
It's got a groove, it's got a mean - ing.
Bm
Em7
To Coda
Grease is the time, is the place, is the mo - tion. Grease is the way we are feel -
1.
G
ing.
2.
G
A
ing.

Bridge:
Em7
F♯m7
G
This is a life of il - lu - sion wrapped up in trou - bles, laced in con - fu -
F♯
Bm
D.S. 𝄋 al Coda
𝄌 Coda
G
A
Bm
sion. What are we do - ing here?
ing.
cresc.
f
N.C.
Grease
(Drum groove continues)
mf

Bm
Em7
— is the word, is the word — that you've heard. It's got a groove, it's got a mean - ing.
Bm
Grease is the time, is the place, is the mo - tion.
Em7
G
Grease is the way we are feel - ing.
Grease
Bm
Fade out
— is the word, is the word, is the word, is the word, is the word, is the word...

GREATEST LOVE OF ALL

1.3.
C#m7
F#m7
Bm7
E7
sense of pride, to make it eas - i - er; let the chil - dren's
place to be, and so I
1st time: D.S. 𝄋
2nd time: To Next Strain
2.
C#m7
F#m7
Bm7
D/E
Bm7
D/E
laugh - ter re - mind us how we used to learned to de - pend on
D(9)
A/C#
Bm7
Bm7/E
me.
be.
I de - cid - ed long a - go nev - er to walk in an - y - one's shad - ow.
mf
D(9)
A/C#
Bm7
Bm7/E
If I fail, if I suc - ceed, at least I lived as I be - lieve. No

D(9)
A/C♯
Bm7
Bm7/E
E/D
mat - ter what they take from me, they can't take a-way my dig - ni - ty. Be - cause the
Chorus:
C♯m7
F♯m7
Bm7
E7
E7/D
C♯m7
F♯m7
Bm7
E7
great - est love of all is hap-pen-ing to me. I found the
C♯m7
F♯m7
Bm7
D/E
A7
great - est love of all in - side of me. The great - est
F♯m7
Bm7
Em7
A7
F♯m7
Bm7
love of all is eas - y to a - chieve.
f

Em7
A7
F♯m7
Bm7
Em7
G/A
Learn - ing to love your - self, it is the great - est love of
dim.
1.
D.S. 𝄋
2.
D
E7
C♯m7
F♯m7
all.
all. And if by chance that spe - cial place
dim.
mf
Bm7
E7
C♯m7
F♯m7
Bm7
E7
that you've been dream - ing of
leads you to a
C♯m7
F♯m7
Bm7
D/E
D(9)
A/C♯
Bm7
E7sus
A(9)
lone - ly place, find your strength in love.
rit. e dim.

HARD TO SAY I'M SORRY

Words and Music by
DAVID FOSTER and PETER CETERA

E♭ Gm7

E - ven lov - ers need a hol - i - day,
Would - n't wan - na be swept a - way,

A♭ E♭/B♭ B♭ Cm7 Fm7

far a - way from each oth - er. Hold me now, it's
far a - way from the one that I love. Hold me now, it's

A♭/B♭ E♭ Cm7 Fm7 B♭ B♭7

hard for me to say I'm sor - ry. I just want you to stay.
hard for me to say I'm sor - ry. I just want you to know.

1.

E♭ A♭/C B♭/D G/B Cm F/A

And af - ter all that you've been through, I will make it up to you, I prom-

A♭/B♭
B♭
B♭7
E♭
A♭/C
B♭/D
G/B
- ise you.
And af - ter all that's been said and done, you're just
Csus
C/B♭
F7/A
B♭sus
B♭
B♭sus
B♭
a part of me I can't let go.
2.
Cm7
Fm7
E♭/B♭
B♭
E♭
Hold me now, I real - ly want to tell you I'm sor - ry.
Cm7
Fm7
B♭
B♭/A♭
I could nev - er let you go, ah.

G♭
C♭/E♭
D♭/F
B♭/D
After all that we've been through, I will make it up
E♭m
A♭7/C
G♭/D♭
D♭
D♭7
G♭
C♭/E♭
to you. I prom - ise to. And af - ter all that's been said
D♭/F
B♭/D
E♭m7
A♭7/C
and done, you're just a part of me I can't let
B♭7sus
B♭7
E♭
go, I can't let go.

HOPELESSLY DEVOTED TO YOU

Words and Music by
JOHN FARRAR

Bm7
E7
Amaj7
A6
eyes are not the first to cry. I'm
sit a-round and wait for you. But,
heart is say-in', "Don't let go.
A
F♯7
C♯m7(♭5)/G
F♯7
not the first to know there's just no get-tin' o - ver
ba - by, can't you see there's noth - in' else for me to
Hold on to the end." And that's what I in - tend to
1.
Bm7
C♯m7
Cm7
Bm7
E7
you.
2. I
2.3.
Bm7
C♯m7
Cm7
Bm7
E13
do?
do.
I'm hope - less - ly de - vot - ed to

Dm
A
you.
But now there's
cresc.
Chorus:
Gm7
C7
no - where to hide since you pushed my love a - side. I'm
f
F
Fmaj7
Adim7
D7(♭9)
out of my head, hope - less - ly de - vot - ed to
Gm7
C13(♭9)
you, hope - less - ly de - vot - ed to

Dm
Dm/C♯
Dm/C
G(9)/B
Bm7(♭5)
you,
1.
Gm7
C13(♭9)
hope - less - ly de - vot - ed to you.
decresc.
mf
A
D.S. 𝄋
2.
Gm7
C13(♭9)
3. My hope - less - ly de - vot - ed to
B♭m
F
you.

HOTEL CALIFORNIA

Optional Guitar Capo 7 → Em B7 D A C G Am

Concert key → Bm F♯7 A E G D Em

Words and Music by
DON HENLEY, GLENN FREY
and DON FELDER

Moderate rock ♩ = 76

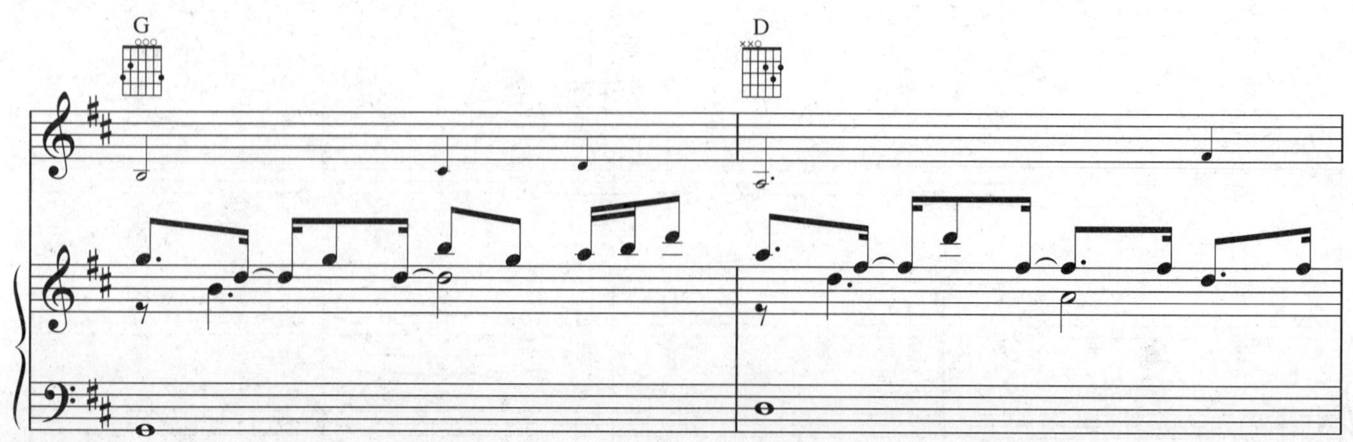

1.
2.
Em
F♯7
F♯7
Verses 1 & 2:
Bm
F♯7
1. On a dark des-ert high-way,
cool wind in my hair,
2. Her mind is Tif - fa - ny twist - ed,
she got the Mer - ce - des bends.
mf
A
E
warm_ smell of co-li - tas_
ris - ing up through the air._
She got a lot of pret-ty, pret-ty boys_
that she calls friends._
G
D
Up a - head in the dis - tance,
I saw a shim-mer - ing light.
How they dance in the court - yard,
sweet_ sum-mer sweat.

Em
F♯7
My head grew heav - y and my sight grew dim,
Some dance to re-mem - ber,
I had to stop for the night.
some dance to for - get.
Bm
F♯7
There she stood in the door - way,
So I called up the cap - tain,
I heard the mis - sion bell.
"Please bring me my wine."
He said,
A
E
And I was think - ing to my - self, "This could be heav - en or this could be hell."
"We have - n't had that spir - it here since nine - teen six - ty - nine.
G
D
Then she lit up a can - dle
And still those voic - es are call - ing from far
and she showed me the way.
a - way,

Em
F#7
There were voic - es down the cor - ri - dor,
I thought I heard them say,
wake you up in the mid - dle of the night
just to hear them say,
Chorus:
G
D
"Wel - come to the Ho - tel Cal - i - for - nia!
Such a
F#7
Bm
love - ly place, (such a love - ly place,) such a love - ly face.
They're
G
D
Plen - ty of room at the Ho - tel Cal - i - for - nia,
an - y
liv - in' it up at the Ho - tel Cal - i - for - nia.
What a

Em
1.
F♯7
time_ of year_ (an - y time_ of year_) you can find_ it here._
nice_ sur - prise,_ (what a nice_ sur - prise,_) bring your
2.
F♯7
N.C.
Verse 3:
Bm
al - i - bis._
Mir - rors_ on the ceil - ing,
mp
F♯7
A
the pink cham - pagne on ice,_ and she said, "We are all just pris - on - ers here_
E
G
of our own_ de - vice." And in the mas - ter's_ cham - bers,

D
Em
they gath-ered for the feast.
They stab it with their steel - y knives, but they
F♯7
Bm
just can't kill the beast.
Last thing I re-mem - ber, I was
F♯7
A
run-ning for the door.
I had to find the pas-sage back to the
E
G
place I was be-fore.
"Re-lax," said the night-man.
"We are

D
Em
— pro - grammed_ to re - ceive.
You can check out an - y - time you like,
F♯7
N.C.
Solo:
Bm
but you can__ nev - er leave."__
(Inst. solo ad lib.…
(Cue notes 2nd time only)
F♯7
A
E
G
D
Em

1.2.
F♯7
3.
F♯7
…end solo)
Bm
F♯7
A
E
G
D
Em
F♯7
Repeat and fade

HOW SOON IS NOW?

Words and Music by
STEVEN MORRISSEY
and JOHNNY MARR

of noth - ing in par - tic - u - lar.
...end solo)
Chorus:
G
A
A
B
A2
B2
C
D
1.2.6. You shut your mouth._
3.4.5. See additional lyrics
G
A
A2
B2
Bsus
C♯sus
D2
E2
How can you say I go a - bout things the wrong
E
F♯
A2
B2
C
D
way? I am hu - man and I need to be loved

To Coda
G A2 Bsus D2
A B2 C♯sus E2
just like ev - 'ry - bod - y else does.
E
F♯
G A E
A B F♯
1.
2.3.
4.
D.S. 𝄋 al Coda
G A G A G A
A B A B A B
2. I am the

Chorus 3:
There's a club if you'd like to go.
You could meet somebody who really loves you.
So you go and you stand on your own.
And you leave on your own, and you go home.
And you cry, and you want to die.

Chorus 4:
When you say it's gonna happen "now,"
Well, when exactly do you mean?
See, I've already waited too long,
And all my hope is gone.

Chorus 5:
(Instrumental)

HOW DEEP IS YOUR LOVE

Words and Music by
BARRY GIBB, MAURICE GIBB
and ROBIN GIBB

Fm7/B♭
E♭
Gm7
Cm7
And the mo - ment that you wan-der far___ from me,___ I wan-na
You're the light___ in my___ deep-est, dark - est hour.___ You're my
Na na na___ na na na na na na___ na na___ na na
feel you in my arms a - gain.___ And you come___ to me___ on a sum-
Sav - iour___ when I fall.___ And you may___ not think___ I___ care___
na___ na na na na na.___ And you come___ to me___ on a sum-
Fm7
Fm7/B♭
A♭maj7
mer breeze,___ keep me warm___ in your love,___ then you soft -
___ for you,___ when you know___ down in - side___ that I real -
mer breeze,___ keep me warm___ in your love___ then you soft -
Gm7
Fm7
ly leave.___
ly do.___
ly leave.___
And it's me you need___ to show;___
How deep___
how deep is your love.
D♭9
Gm7
A♭maj7/B♭

Chorus:
E♭
E♭maj7
A♭maj7
__ is your love,__ how deep__ is your__ love? I real - ly mean__ to learn._
A♭m6
E♭
B♭m/A♭
__ 'Cause we're liv - ing in a world of fools,__ break - ing us
C7
Fm7
1.2.
A♭m6
down when they all__ should let us be.__ We be - long__ to you__ and me.
3.
A♭m6
E♭
Gm7
A♭maj7/B♭
D.S. and fade
__ to you__ and me. Na na na na na.__ How deep_

HUMAN NATURE

Words and Music by
JEFF PORCARO and JOHN BETTIS

G
A
G
A
time,
the cit - y winks a sleep - less eye.
G
A
G
Hear her voice
shake my win -
A
G
F♯m7
Em7
Asus4
dow:
sweet, se - duc - ing sighs.
G
A
G
A
Get me out in - to the night -
Reach - ing out to touch a stran -
Look - ing out a - cross the morn -

G
A
G
A
time. Four walls won't hold me to-night.
ger, e-lec-tric eyes are ev-'ry-where.
ing, the cit-y's heart be-gins to beat.
G
A
G
If this town is just an ap-
See that girl? She knows I'm watch-
Reach-ing out, I touch her shoul-
A
G
F#m7
Em7
ple, then let me take a bite.
ing. She likes the way I stare.
der. I'm dream-ing of the street.

A
G
A
D
D/C♯
If they_ say, "Why, why?" tell 'em that_ it's hu -
Bm7
A
G
F♯m7
Em7
man na - ture. Why, why does he do me that way?
Bm
G
A
D
D/C♯
If they_ say, "Why, why?" tell 'em that_ it's hu -
Bm7
A
G
F♯m7
To Coda
man na - ture. Why, why does he

1.
Em7
A
2.
Em7
do me that way?
do me that way?
Bm
Em7
Bm
I like liv - in' this way.
I like
Em7
Bm
Em9
lov - in' this way.
Gmaj7/A
2fr.
G(addA)
A

Fmaj7
Em7
G(addA)
A
Fmaj7
Em7
D. S. al Coda
Coda
Em9
do me that way?
Gmaj7/A
2 fr.
G(addA)
A
I like liv - in' this way.
Fmaj7
Em7

G(addA)
A
Fmaj7
Em7
B♭maj7
Am7
Fmaj7
Em7
B♭maj7
Repeat and fade
B♭maj7

THEME FROM "ICE CASTLES"

(Through the Eyes of Love)

Lyrics by
CAROLE BAYER SAGER

Music by
MARVIN HAMLISCH

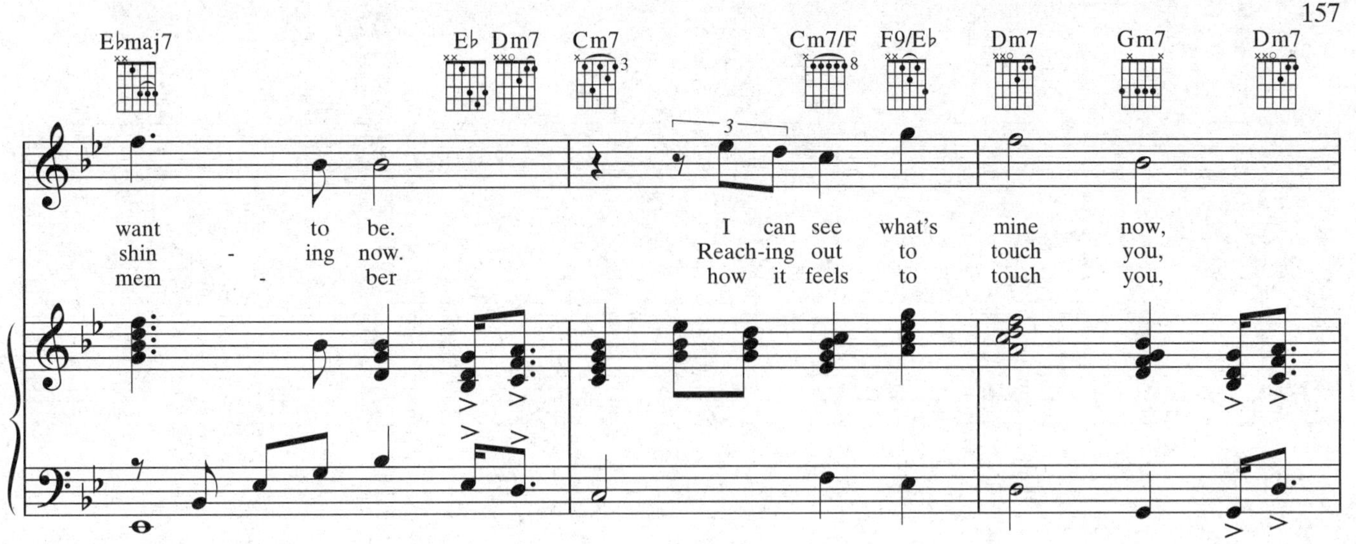
Ebmaj7
Eb Dm7
Cm7
Cm7/F
F9/Eb
Dm7
Gm7
Dm7
want to be. I can see what's mine now,
shin - ing now. Reach-ing out to touch you,
mem - ber how it feels to touch you,

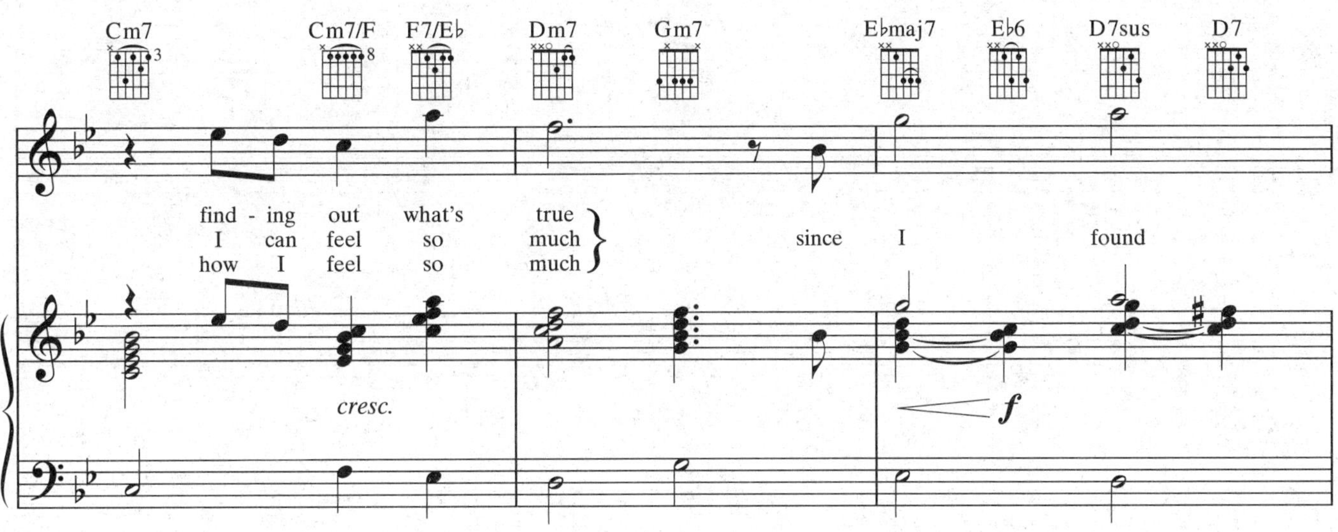
Cm7
Cm7/F
F7/Eb
Dm7
Gm7
Ebmaj7
Eb6
D7sus
D7
find - ing out what's true
I can feel so much
how I feel so much
since I found
cresc.
f

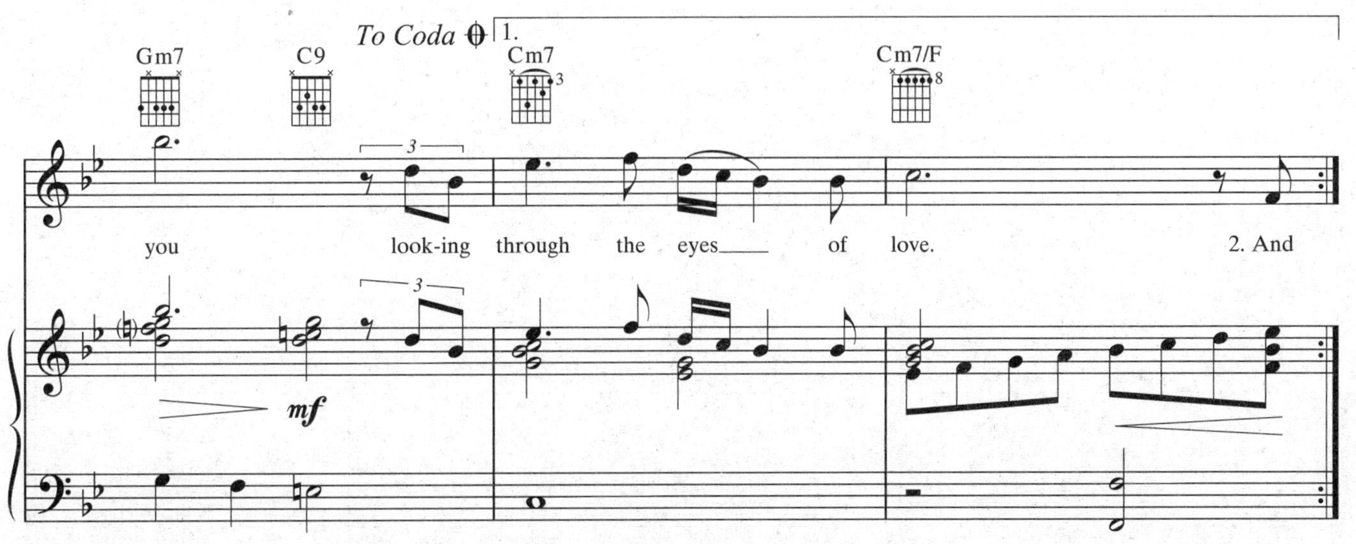
To Coda
1.
Gm7
C9
Cm7
Cm7/F
you look-ing through the eyes of love. 2. And
mf

2.
Cm7
Cm7/F
B♭
Gm7
through the eyes___ of love. And now I
f
Dm7
Gm7
Dm7
Cm7
Cm7/F
B♭maj7
do be - lieve that e - ven in the storm we'll find___ some light.
Cm7
Dm7
E♭
C7
Cm7/F
Know - ing you're be - side me I'm all___ right.______
mf
cresc.
f
mf
D.S. 𝄋 al Coda
𝄌 Coda
Cm7
Cm7/F
B♭
through the eyes___ of love.
mf rit.

ISLANDS IN THE STREAM

Words and Music by
BARRY GIBB, MAURICE GIBB
and ROBIN GIBB

C
real thing.
You do some - thing to me that I
But that won't hap - pen to us and we
can't ex - plain;
hold me clos - er and I feel no pain. Ev - 'ry
got no doubt;
too deep in love, and we got no way out. And the
Fsus2
C
beat of my heart, we got some - thing go - ing on.
mes - sage is clear; this could be the year of the real thing.
Fsus2
Ten - der love is blind; it re - quires a ded - i - ca - tion. All
No more will you cry; ba - by, I will hurt you nev - er. We

Fm6/A♭
6fr
C
this love we feel needs no con - ver - sa - tion. We ride it to - geth - er, uh -
start and end as one, in love for - ev - er. We can ride it to - geth - er, uh -
huh, from one love to an - oth - er, uh - huh. (1.,2.) Is - lands in
huh, from one love to an - oth - er, uh - huh.
C
F
Dm7
the stream, that is what we are. No one in be - tween; how can we
(3.) per - star; that is what you are, com - ing from a - far, reach - ing for
C
F
be wrong? Get a - way with me to an - oth - er world, and we re -
the stars. Far a - way with me to an - oth - er place, and we re -

C
1
Dm7
Dm7/G
ly on each oth - er, uh - huh, from one lov - er to an - oth - er, uh -
ly on each oth - er, uh - huh, from one lov -
C
Em
Fsus2
Gsus
3fr
D.S.
huh.
2
Dm7
Dm7/G
C
Em
- er to an - oth - er, uh - huh.
Fsus2
Gsus
3fr
C
Em
I'll ___ be al -

3
Fsus2
Gsus
3fr
Dm7
Dm7/G
-right, oh. Get 'em, su - - er to an - oth - er, uh -
C
Em
Fsus2
huh. I'll be al - right. Good - bye, to - night.
Gsus
3fr
C
Em
Good - night for now. Good - bye, to - night.
Fsus2
C/G
Gsus
3fr
C
Al - right, for now good - bye.

IF YOU DON'T KNOW ME BY NOW

Words and Music by
KENNETH GAMBLE and LEON HUFF

* Background vocals sung at pitch.

E♭ Cm7/F F Gm7 F7/A

you should un - der - stand me like I un - der - stand you.

B♭ Dm7

Now, girl, I know the dif - f'rence be - tween right and wrong.

E♭ Cm7/F F Gm7 F7/A

I ain't gon - na do noth - in' to break up our hap - py home.

D♭ G♭maj7

Oh, don't get so ex - cit - ed when I come home a lit - tle late at night,

E♭m7
Cm7/F
F
Gm7
F7/A
'cause we on - ly act like chil - dren
when we ar - gue, fuss, and fight.
Chorus:
B♭
Dm7
(Bkgrd.) (If you don't know me by now,
If you don't know me,
you will
E♭
E♭m6/G♭
nev - er, nev - er, nev - er know me.
No, you won't.
Ooh.)
B♭
Dm7
(If you don't know me by now,
you will

E♭ Ebm6/G♭

nev - er, nev - er, nev - er know_ me. Ooh.______)

Verse 2:

B♭ Dm7

2. We've all got our own fun - ny moods.______

E♭ Cm7/F F Gm7 F7/A

I got mine;_ wom - an, you got yours too.

B♭ Dm7

Just trust in me like I trust in you.______

E♭
Cm7/F
F
Gm7
F7/A
As long as we've been to-geth-er,
it should be so eas - y to do.
D♭
G♭maj7
just get your-self to-geth-er,
or we might as well say good-bye.
E♭m7
Cm7/F
F
Gm7
F7/A
What good is a love af-fair
when you can't see eye to eye?
Chorus:
B♭
Dm7
(If you don't know me by now,
If you don't know me,
you will

E♭
E♭m6/G♭
B♭
No, you won't.
nev-er, nev-er, nev-er know_ me.
Ooh.
(If you don't know me by
Dm7
E♭
you
will nev-er, nev-er, nev-er know me.
now,
you will nev-er, nev-er, nev-er know_ me.
E♭m6/G♭
B♭
Ooh.
)
(If you don't know me by
Dm7
E♭
E♭m6/G♭
Mm.
now,
you will nev-er, nev-er, nev-er know_ me.
Ooh.)

JUMP

Words and Music by
EDWARD VAN HALEN, ALEX VAN HALEN,
MICHAEL ANTHONY and DAVID LEE ROTH

F/C
C
F/C
C/F
Gsus4
G/C
3 fr.
C
F/C
G/C
3 fr.
I get up,
and noth - ing gets me
C
F/C
C/F
Gsus4
G/C
3 fr.
C
down.
You got it tough.
F/C
G/C
3 fr.
C
F/C
C/F
Gsus4
I seen the tough - est soul a - round.
And I

G/C C F/C G/C C F/C
know, ba - by, just how you feel.
C/F Gsus4 G/C C F/C G/C
You got to roll with the punch - es to get to what's
C F/C C/F Gsus4 Am
real. Ah, can't you see me stand - ing here? I got my
F C/E Dm
back a - gainst the rec - ord ma - chine. I ain't the worst that you've seen.

F
C/E
Dm
F
C/E
G
Ah, can't you see what I mean?
G/C
C
Ah, might as well jump.
F/C
G/C
C
F/C
C/F
Gsus4
To Coda
Might as well jump.
Go a - head and jump.
G/C
C
F/C
G/C
F/C
C
F/C
Go a - head and jump.

C/F
Gsus4
G/C
C
F/C
G/C
3 fr.
How old___ are you?_ Who said that?___ Ba - by, how_ you been?_
C
F/C
C/F
Gsus4
G/C
C
You say you don't know.___ You won't
F/C
G/C
C
F/C
C/F
Gsus4
D. S. al Coda
know_ un - til you be - gin.__ So can't you
Coda
G/C
C
F/C
G/C
C
F/C
Go a - head and jump._

C/F
Gsus4
B♭m
G♭
A♭
4 fr.
D♭
Jump!
G/C
3 fr.
C
F/C
G/F
F

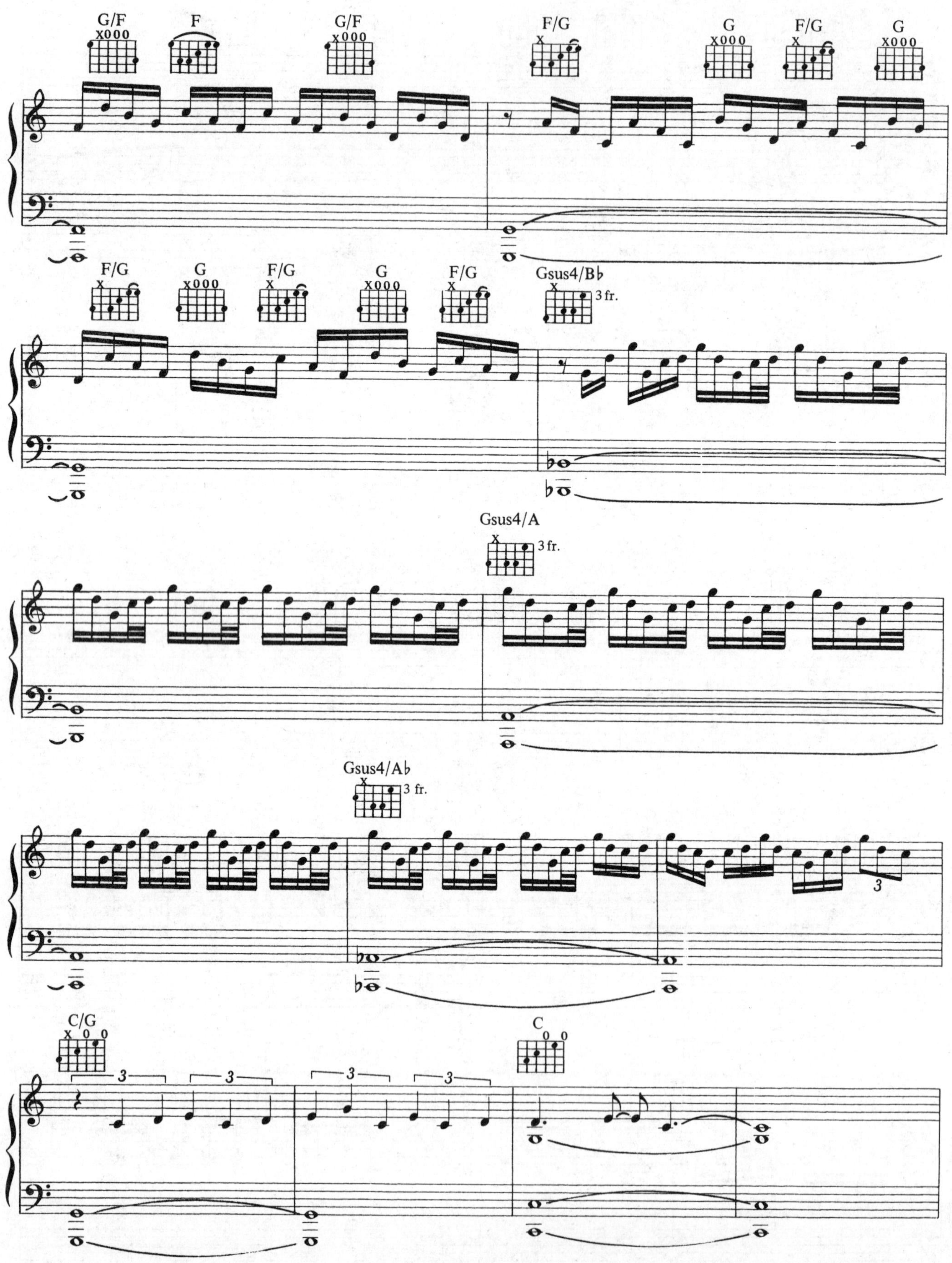
G/F
F
G/F
F/G
G
F/G
G
F/G
G
F/G
G
F/G
Gsus4/B♭
3 fr.
Gsus4/A
3 fr.
Gsus4/A♭
3 fr.
C/G
C

G/C
C
F/C
3 fr.
C/F
Gsus4
Repeat and fade
Might as well jump.
Go a - head and jump.
Might as well

KISS ON MY LIST

Words and Music by
DARYL HALL and JANNA ALLEN

C(add9)
Cm7
You think may - be I need help
me.
Some - times I for - get what I'm do -
Fm
no, I know I'm right all right I'm
- ing, I don't for - get what I want I want re -
Ab
Ab/Bb
C(add9)
just bet - ter off not lis - ten - ing to friends' ad - vice
gret what I've done re - gret you, I could - n't go on
Fm7
Gsus/D
when they in - sist on know - ing my bliss
but if you in - sist on know - ing my bliss

Fm7
Gsus/D
Fm7
I tell them this when they want to know what the rea - son is
I'll tell you this if you want to know what the rea - son is
Gsus/D
Fm7
F/G
G7
CHORUS
I on - ly smile when I lie, then I tell them why
I'll on - ly smile when I lie, then I'll tell you why
Be-cause your
C
G/C
F/C
G/C
Cm7
B♭/C
kiss (Your kiss) is on my list, be - cause your kiss (your kiss) is on
Cm7
F
my list be - cause your kiss is on my list of the best things in life.

G/C
C
G
C
G/C
C
G/C
Be - cause your kiss (your kiss) is on
F/C
G/C
Cm7
B♭/C
Cm7
my list, be - cause your kiss (your kiss) I can't re - sist be - cause your
F
1
C
kiss is what I miss when I turn out the light.
2,3
C
D.S. twice (Fade 2nd time)
(2) I go
Be - cause your

MARGARITAVILLE

Words and Music by
JIMMY BUFFETT

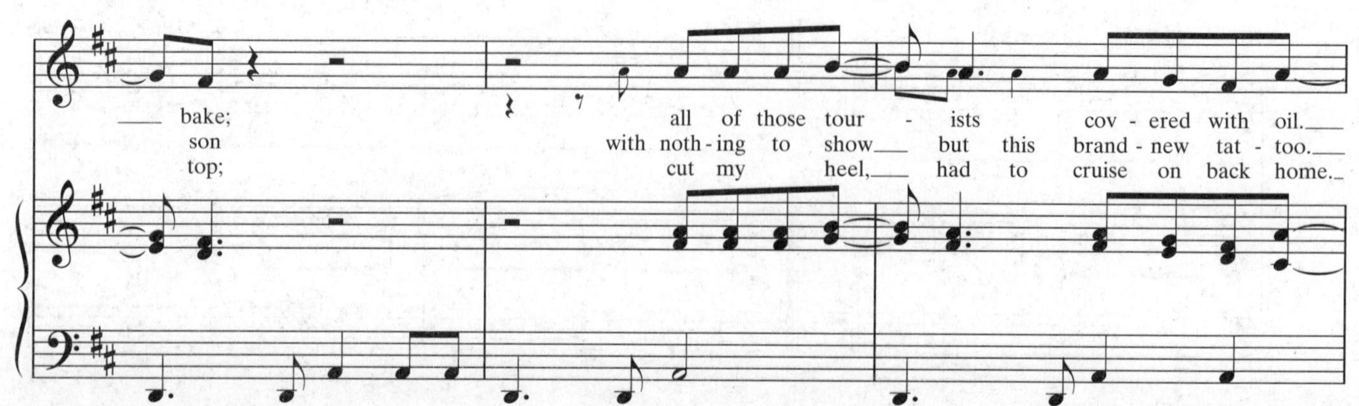

A
Strum-min' my six - string
But it's a real beau - ty,
But there's booze in the blend - er,
on my front porch swing.
a Mex - i - can cu - tie,
and soon it will ren - der
Smell those shrimp;
how it got
that fro - zen con -
D
they're be - gin - ning to boil.
here I have - n't a clue.
coc - tion that helps me hang on.
Chorus:
G
A
D
D7
Wast-in' a - way a - gain in Mar - ga - ri - ta - ville,

G
A
D
searchin' for my lost shak - er of salt.
D7
G
A
Some people claim that there's a
D
A/C♯
G
A
wom - an to blame,
but I know
now I think,
but I know
1.2.
D
it's no - bod - y's fault.
hell, it could be my fault.
it's my own damn fault.

3.
D
G
Yes, and some people claim that there's a wom - an to blame, and I know
A
D
A/C♯
G
it's my own damn fault.
A
D
G
A
D

SONG FROM "M*A*S*H"
(Suicide Is Painless)

Words and Music by
MIKE ALTMAN and JOHNNY MANDEL

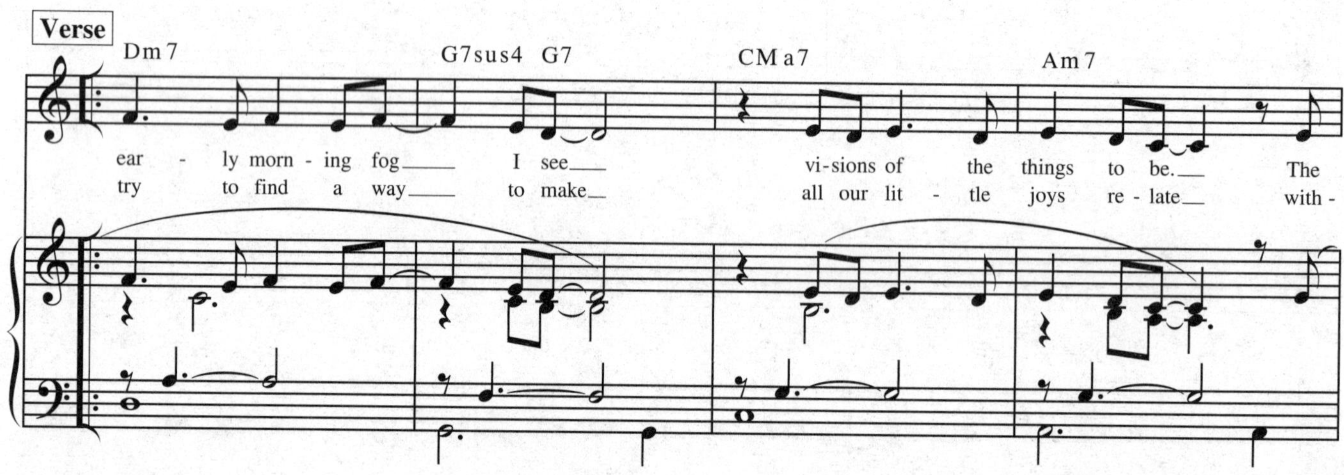

Am7
G/A
A7
can see
too late
that
and
Chorus
Dm7
G7
C(add2)
Am7
su - i - cide is pain - less. It brings on man - y chang - es and
FMa7
C/E
Dm7
Dm7/G
1. 2. 3. 4. & 5.
Am
Am9
Am
G/A
I can take or leave it if I please.
I
6.
Am
Am9
Am
G/A
and
rall....
poco a poco molto rall.

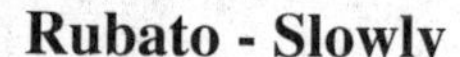

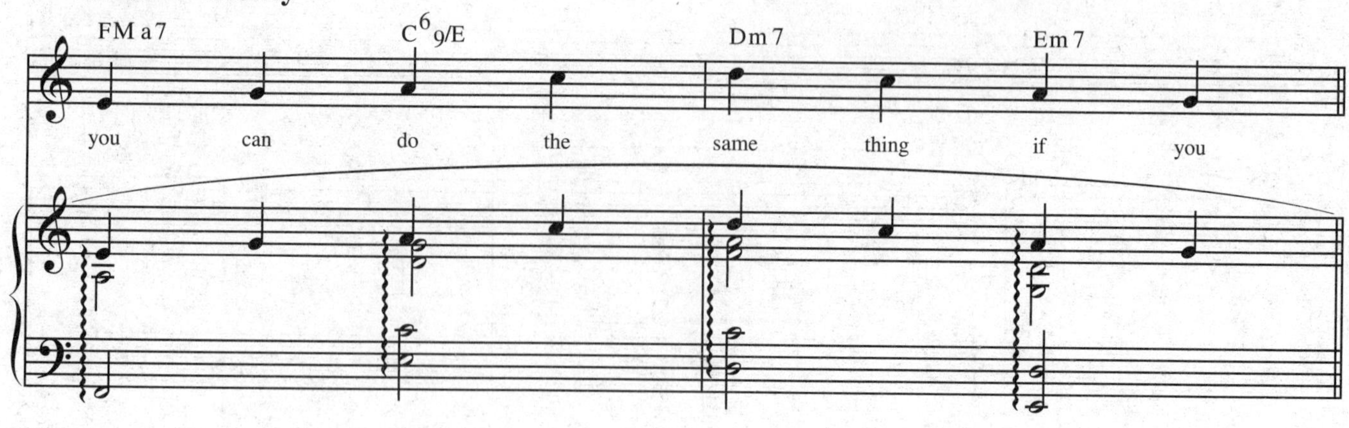

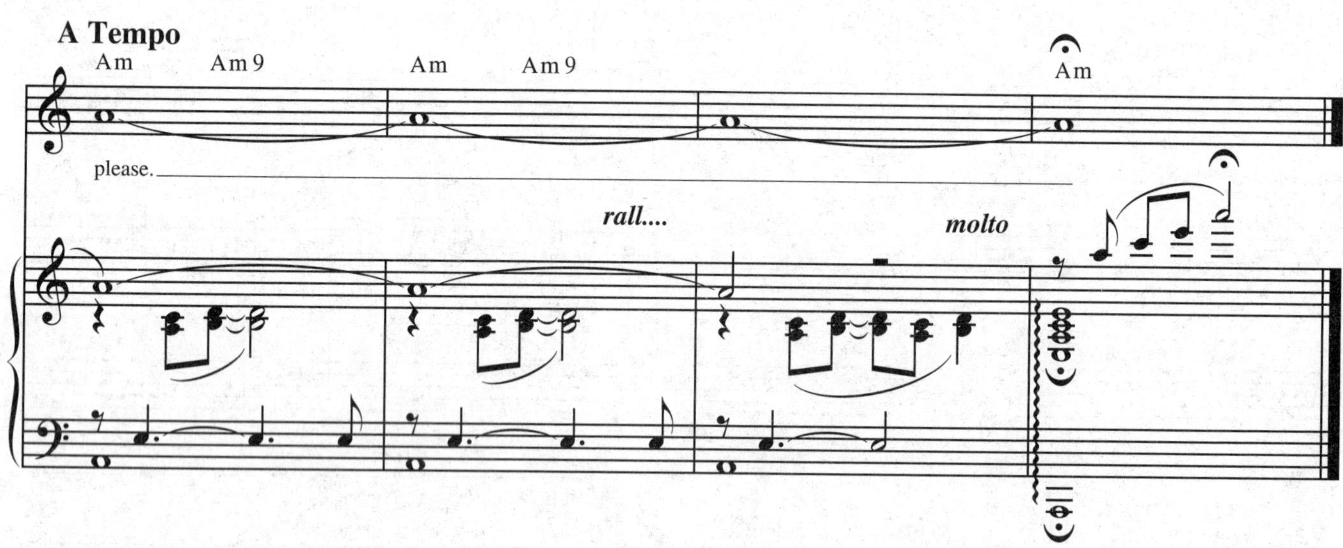

3. The game of life is hard to play.
   I'm going to lose it anyway.
   The losing card I'll someday lay,
   so this is all I have to say.
   That: (chorus)

4. The only way to win, is cheat
   and lay it down before I'm beat,
   and to another give a seat
   for that's the only painless feat.
   'Cause (chorus)

5. The sword of time will pierce our skins.
   It doesn't hurt when it begins,
   but as it works its way on in,
   the pain grows stronger, watch it grin.
   For: (chorus)

6. A brave man once requested me
   to answer questions that are key.
   Is it to be or not to be?
   And I replied; "Oh, why ask me?"
   'Cause (chorus)

MOONDANCE

Words and Music by
VAN MORRISON
Jazz shuffle ♩ = 132
Am7
Bm7
mf
Verse:
1. Well, it's a
(4.) mar - vel - ous night for a moon -
(2.) wan - na make love to you to -
(3.) (Inst. solo ad lib....
dance with the stars up a - bove in your eyes, a fan -
night, I can't wait 'til the morn - ing has come. And I

Am7
Bm7
tab - u - lous night to make ro - mance 'neath the cov - er of Oc - to - ber
know now the time is just right and straight in - to my arms you will
skies. And all the leaves on the trees are fall - ing to the
run. And when you come, my heart will be wait - ing to make
sound of the breez - es that blow. And I'm try - ing to please to the call -
sure that you're nev - er a - lone. There and then all my dreams will come true,
ing of your heart - strings that play soft and low. And all the
dear, there and then will I make you my own. And ev - 'ry
3

Dm6
Am7
Dm6
night's mag - ic seems to whis - per and hush,
time I touch you, you just trem - ble in - side.
Am7
Dm6
Am7
and all the soft moon - light seems to
And I know how much you want me
N.C.
Dm6
N.C.
E7(♯5)
Am7
shine in your blush.
that you can't hide.
Can I
Chorus:
Dm7
Am7
Dm7
Am7
just have one more moon - dance with you,

Dm7
Am7
Dm7
Am7
Dm7
Am7
my love? Can I just make some more
Dm7
Am7
Dm7
Am7
1.2.3.
E7
ro - mance with you, my love?
2. Well, I
3. (Inst. solo ad lib....
4. It's a
4.
E7
Am7
Bm7
Am7
Bm7
One more moon - dance with you in the
Am7
Bm7
Am7
Bm7
Am7
Bm7
moon - light on a mag - ic night.

Am7
Bm7
La la la la, in the
moon - light on a mag - ic night.
Am
Em/G
Fmaj7
Em7
Can't I just have one more moon - dance with
Dm7
N.C.
Am9
you, my love?

NOTHING'S GONNA STOP US NOW

Words and Music by
DIANE WARREN and ALBERT HAMMOND

Dm7
Bb
C
so much to give you this love in my heart that I'm feel - ing for you.
you through the bad times, what-ev - er it takes is what I'm gon-na do.
F
Dm7
Let them say we're cra - zy, I don't care a-bout that.
Let them say we're cra - zy, what do they know.
Bb
C
Put your hand in my hand, ba - by, don't ev - er look back.
Put your arms a - round me, ba - by, don't ev - er let go.
F
Dm7
Let the world a - round us just fall a - part.

B♭
E♭
C
Ba - by, we can make it if we're heart to heart.
And we can build
F
Dm7
B♭
this dream to - geth - er, stand - ing strong for - ev - er, noth - ing's gon - na stop us now.
mf
C
F
Dm7
And if this world runs out of lov - ers we'll still have each oth - er, noth -
B♭
1. C
To Coda
2. C
ing's gon - na stop us, noth - ing's gon - na stop us. I'm ing's gon - na stop us.

F
C/F
F
Bb
Oh,
all that I need is you,
Gm7
3fr.
C
F
F/C
F
you're all I ev - er need.
All that I want to do
Bb
Gm7
3fr.
is hold you for - ev - er,
for -
C7
C
D.S. al Coda
ev - er and ev - er.
And we can build

Repeat and fade (lead vocal ad-lib)
Coda
C
F
Dm7
ing's gon - na stop us.
(And we can build) this dream to - geth - er, stand - ing strong for - ev - er, noth -
B♭
C
F
ing's gon - na stop us now. And if this world runs out of lov - ers, we'll
Dm7
B♭
C
still have each oth - er, noth - ing's gon - na stop us, noth - ing's gon - na stop us.
(And we can build

PIANO IN THE DARK

Words and Music by
BRENDA RUSSELL, JEFF HULL
and SCOTT CUTLER

Fm(addG)
E♭6
Cm7
3fr.
I nev - er think a - bout all the fun - ny things you've said;
D♭6
4fr.
D♭
4fr.
A♭/C
D♭
4fr.
E♭
I feel like it's dead. The feel-ings in me now.
Fm(addG)
E♭6
Cm7
3fr.
I turn a - round in the still of the room
He holds me close like a beat of a heart.
Fm(addG)
E♭6
Cm7
3fr.
D♭6
4fr.
D♭
4fr.
know-ing this is when I'm gon - na make my move. Can't
He plays the mel - o - dy, want to tear me all a - part. The

A♭/C
C7+5
3fr.
B♭/D
C/E
wait an - y long - er and I'm feel - ing strong - er.
si - lence is bro - ken and no words are spo - ken.
But oh,
F
B♭
F/C
B♭/D
just as I walk to the door I can feel your e - mo -
F
B♭
F/C
B♭/D
tion there. It's pull - ing me back, back to love you.
Dm7
B♭
F/C
C
Gm7
3fr.
F/A
Oh, no, caught up in the mid - dle, I cry just a lit - tle when

B♭
C
Dm7
B♭
F/C
C
I think of let - ting go.
Oh, no,
gave up on the rid - dle, I cry
Gm7
3fr.
F/A
B♭m9
C7+5
3fr.
To Coda
1.
Fm
just a lit - tle when he plays pi - an - o in the dark.
D♭
4fr.
A♭/C
D♭
4fr.
E♭
2.
Fm(addG)
the dark.
3
E♭6
Cm7
3fr.
Fm(addG)
E♭6
Cm7
3fr.
D♭6
4fr.
D♭
4fr.
Oh, the

A♭/C C7+5 B♭/D C/E

D.S. 𝄋 al Coda 𝄌

si - lence is bro - ken and no words are spo - ken. But oh,

𝄌 *Coda*

Fm E♭6 Cm7 3fr.

the dark.

Fm E♭6 Cm7 3fr. Fm

1. E♭6 Cm7 3fr.

2. E♭6 Cm7 3fr. Fm

OPEN ARMS

Words and Music by
JONATHAN CAIN and STEVE PERRY

D
A/C♯
G(9)/B
Soft - ly you whis - per; you're so sin - cere.
Want - ing to hold you, want - ing you near;
Bm
A
G
Em
How could our love be so blind? We sailed on to -
how much I want - ed you home. But now that you've
mf
Bm
A/C♯
D
geth - er, we drift - ed a - part, and here you
come back, turned night in - to day, I
A
G
A/G
G
A/G
are by my side.
need you to stay.
So, now I

Chorus:
D
D(9)/F♯
come to you with o - pen arms;
f
G
C9
noth - ing to hide, be - lieve what I say. So,
D(9)
D
D(9)/F♯
here I am with o - pen arms;
G
C9
hop - ing you see what your love means to me, o - pen

1.
D
A/C♯
G(9)/B
arms.
p
Bm
A
G
2.
D
D7/F♯
arms.
mp
G(9)
C9
D
rit. e dim.
hold

RAPPER'S DELIGHT

Words and Music by
BERNARD EDWARDS and NILE RODGERS

Moderate funk ♩ = 112

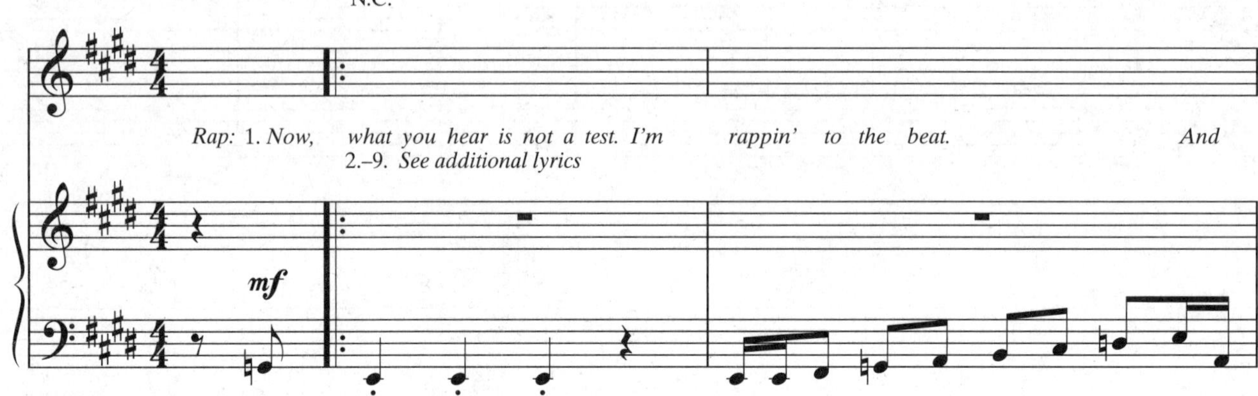

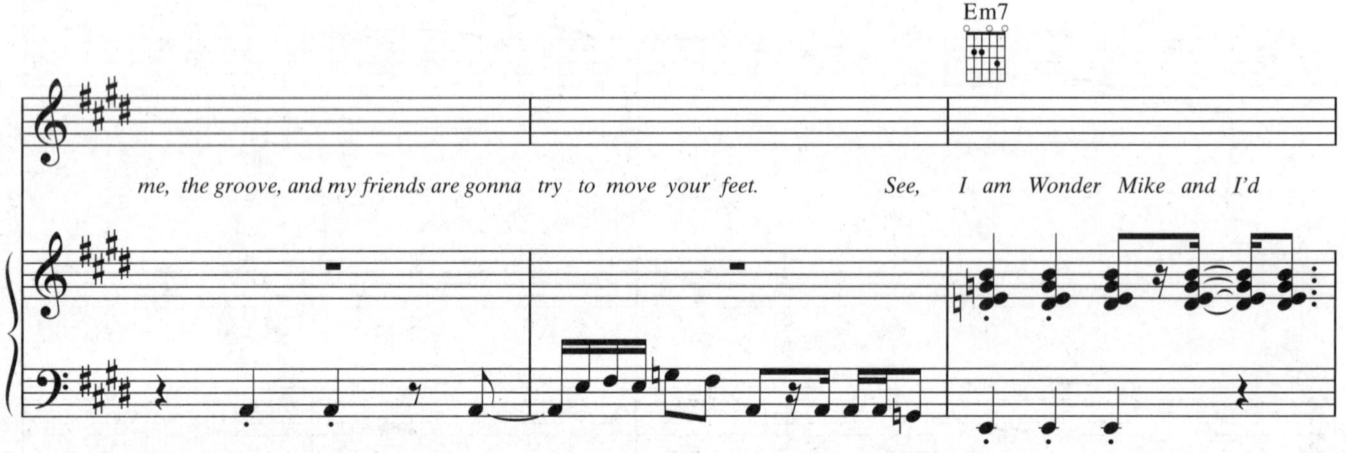

Em7
E7sus
Em7/A
bang-bang the boogie to the boogie. Say up jump the boogie to the bang-bang boogie. Let's rock, you don't stop. Rock the
A6
Em7
N.C.
riddle that will make your body rock. Well, so far you've heard my voice, a-but I brought two friends along. And next
1.–8.
9.
on the mike is my man Hank. Come on Hank, sing that song. 2. Check it out, I'm the rhythm of the boogie, the beat.
Em7
E7sus
Em7/A

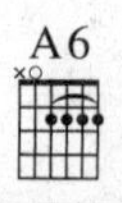

Repeat and fade

Verse 2:
Check it out, I'm the c-a-s-an-the-o-v-a and the rest is f-l-y.
Ya see, I go by the code of the doctor of the mix
and these reasons I'll tell ya why.
Ya see, I'm six foot one and I'm tons of fun and I dress to a "T."
Ya see, I got more clothes than Muhammad Ali and I dress so viciously.
I got bodyguards, I got two big cars that definitely ain't the wack.
I got a Lincoln Continental and a sunroof Cadillac.
So after school, I take a dip in the pool, which really is on the wall.
I got a color TV so I can see the Knicks play basketball.

Verse 3:
Hear me talkin' 'bout checkbooks, credit cards,
more money than a sucker could ever spend.
But I wouldn't give a sucker or a bum from the rucker,
not a dime till I made it again.
Everybody go hotel, motel, whatcha gonna do today? (Say what?)
Ya say I'm gonna get a fly girl, gonna get some spankin',
drive off in a def o-j. Everybody go, hotel, motel, Holiday Inn.
Say if your girl starts actin' up, then you take her friend.
Master Gee, am I mellow. It's on you, so what you gonna do?

Verse 4:
Well, it's on 'n' on 'n' on on 'n' on.
The beat don't stop until the break of dawn.
I said, "M-A-S-T-E-R a G with a double E."
I said, I go by the unforgettable name
of the man they call the Master Gee.
Well, my name is known all over the world
by all the foxy ladies and the pretty girls.
I'm goin' down in history as the baddest rapper there ever could be.
Now, I'm feelin' the highs and ya feelin' the lows,
the beat starts gettin' into your toes.
Ya start poppin' your fingers and stompin' your feet,
and movin' your body while youre sittin' in your seat.
And then, damn, ya start doin' the freak.
I said, damn, right outta your seat.
Then ya throw your hands high in the air,
ya rockin' to the rhythm, shake your derriere.

Verse 5:
Ya rockin' to the beat without a care,
with the sureshot M.C.s for the affair.
Now, I'm not as tall as the rest of the gang,
but I rap to the beat just the same.
I got a little face and a pair of brown eyes.
All I'm here to do, ladies, is hypnotize.
Singin' on 'n' 'n' on 'n' on on 'n' on.
The beat don't stop until the break of dawn.
Singin' on 'n' 'n' on 'n' on on 'n' on,
like a hot buttered a-pop da pop da pop dibbie dibbie
pop da pop pop ya don't dare stop.
Come alive, y'all, gimme what ya got.
I guess by now you can take a hunch
and find that I am the baby of the bunch.
But that's okay, I still keep in stride,
'cause all I'm here to do is just wiggle your behind.

Verse 6.
Singin' on 'n' 'n' on 'n' on on 'n' on.
The beat don't stop until the break of dawn.
Singin' on 'n' 'n' on 'n' on on 'n' on.
Rock, rock, y'all, throw it on the floor.
I'm gonna freak ya here, I'm gonna freak ya there.
I'm gonna move you outta this atmosphere.
'Cause I'm one of a kind and I'll shock your mind.
I'll put t-t-tickets in your behind.
I said, 1-2-3-4, come on, girls, get on the floor.
A-come alive, y'all, a-gimme what ya got,
'cause I'm guaranteed to make you rock.
I said, 1-2-3-4, tell me, Wonder Mike, what are you waitin for?

Verse 7:
I said, a-hip hop the hippie to the hippie
the hip hip hop, a-you don't stop.
The rock it to the bang-bang boogie, say up jumped the boogie,
to the rhythm of the boogie, the beat.
Skiddlee beebop a-we rock a-scoobie doo.
And guess what, America? We love you,
'cause ya rock and ya roll with so much soul.
You could rock till you're a hundred and one years old.
I don't mean to brag, I don't mean to boast,
but we like hot butter on our breakfast toast.
Rock it up, baby bubbah, baby bubbah, to the boogie da
bang bang da boogie to the beat beat, it's so unique.
Come on, everybody, and dance to the beat.

Verse 8:
Ever went over a friend's house to eat,
and the food just ain't no good?
I mean the macaroni's soggy, the peas are mushed,
and the chicken tastes like wood.
So you try to play it off like you think you can,
by sayin' that you're full.
And then your friend says, "Momma, he's just being polite,
he ain't finished, uh-uh, that's bull."
So your heart starts pumpin' and you think of a lie,
and you say that you already ate.
And your friend says, "Man, there's plenty of food."
So you pile some more on your plate.
While the stinky food's steamin', your mind starts to dreamin'
of the moment that it's time to leave.
And then you look at your plate and your chickens slowly rottin'
into something that looks like cheese.
Oh, so you say, "That's it, I got to leave this place.
I don't care what these people think.
I'm just sittin' here makin' myself nauseous
with this ugly food that stinks."

Verse 9:
So you bust out the door while it's still closed,
still sick from the food you ate.
And then you run to the store for quick relief
from a bottle of Kaopectate.
And then you call your friend two weeks later
to see how he has been.
And he says, "I understand about the food, baby bubbah,
but we're still friends." With a hip hop the hippie to the hippie
the hip hip a hop, a-you don't stop the rockin'
to the bang bang boogie.
Say up jump the boogie to the rhythm of the boogie, the beat.

RIGHT HERE WAITING

Words and Music by
RICHARD MARX

Gsus
G
C2
C2/F
slow - ly go in - sane. I hear your voice on the line,
thought would last some - how. I hear the laugh - ter, I taste the
Dm11
G/B
Am
but it does - n't stop the pain. If I see you next
tears, but I can't get near you now. Oh, can't you see
Dm11
Am
Dm11
G7sus
to nev - er, how can we say for - ev - er?
it, ba - by, you've got me go - in' cra - zy?
Chorus:
C
G
Am
Wher - ev - er you go, what - ev - er you do, I will be right

F
G
C
G
here wait - ing for you.
What-ev - er it takes,
or how my heart breaks,
To Coda
1.
Am
F
G
Am
I will be right here wait - ing for you.
2.
Bridge:
F
G
Dm11
here wait - ing for you.
I won - der
C/E
F2
how we can sur - vive this ro - mance.

Dm11
C/E
F2
But in the end if I'm with you, I'll take the chance.
Gsus
C
G
Am
F
G
C
G
Am
F
G
Am
Oh, can't you see

D.S. 𝄋 al Coda
Dm11
Am
Dm11
G7sus
it, ba - by,
you've got me go - in' cra - zy?
Coda
F
G
C
G
here wait - ing for you.
Am
F
G
C
Wait - ing for you.
G
Am
F
Gsus
G
C
rit.

RICH GIRL

Words and Music by
DARYL HALL

Gm7
F/C
Dm7
Gm7
Am7
Dm7
Gm7
Am7
Bbmaj7
Am7
that it's wrong to take what he's giv-in you. So far gone, on your own,
Gm7
Gm7
Dm7
Gm7
Dm7
Bb/C
but you could get a-long if you tried to be strong, but you'll nev-er be strong. You're a
F
Am7
Dm7
F/C
Rich Girl and you've gone too far 'cause you know it does-n't mat-ter an-y-way.
Bb
F/A
Gm7
Bb/C
Bb/D
You can re-ly on the old man's mon-ey, you can re-ly on the old man's mon-ey. It's a
F
Am7
Dm7
F/C
bitch, girl, but it's gone too far 'cause you know it does-n't mat-ter an-y-way.

Bb
F/A
Gm7
F
Gm7
Am7
Say, mon - ey, mon - ey won't get you too far, get you too far.
High and
Bbmaj7
Am7
Gm7
F/C
dry, out of the rain, It's so eas - y to hurt
Gm7
Am7
Dm7
Gm7
Am7
Bbmaj7
Am7
Gm7
oth - ers when you can't feel pain. Don't you know that a love can't grow.
But it's
Dm7
Gm7
Dm
Bb/C
too much to give 'cause you'd rath - er live for the thrill of it all.
You're a
F
Am7
Dm7
F/C
Rich Girl and you've gone too far 'cause you know it does - n't mat - ter an - y - way.

Bb
F/A
Gm7
Bb/C
You can re - ly___ on the old man's mon-ey, you can re - ly___ on the old man's mon-ey. It's a
F
Am7
Dm7
F/C
bitch girl, but it's gone too far 'cause you know it does-n't mat-ter an - y - way.___
Bb
F/A
Bb
Dm7
F
Say, mon - ey, mon-ey won't get you too far, Say, mon - ey, mon-ey won't get you too far,
Bb
F/A
Gm7
F
Say, mon - ey, mon - ey won't get you too far, get you too far.___ And you say___
Bb
F/A
Bb
Repeat and Fade
you can re - ly___ on the old man's mon-ey, you can re - ly___ on the old man's mon - ey. You're a

THE ROSE

Words and Music by
AMANDA McBROOM

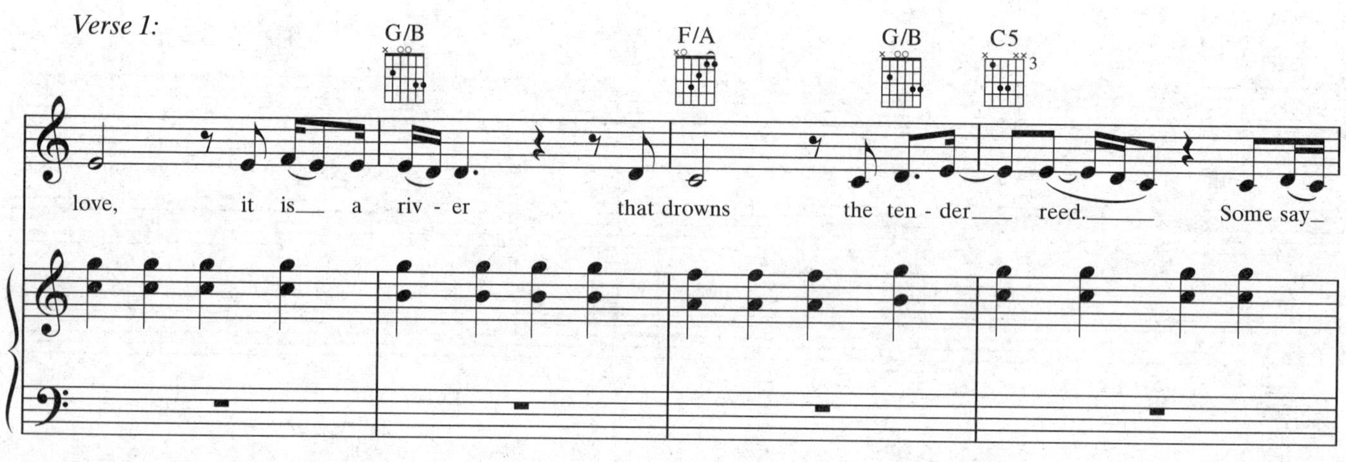

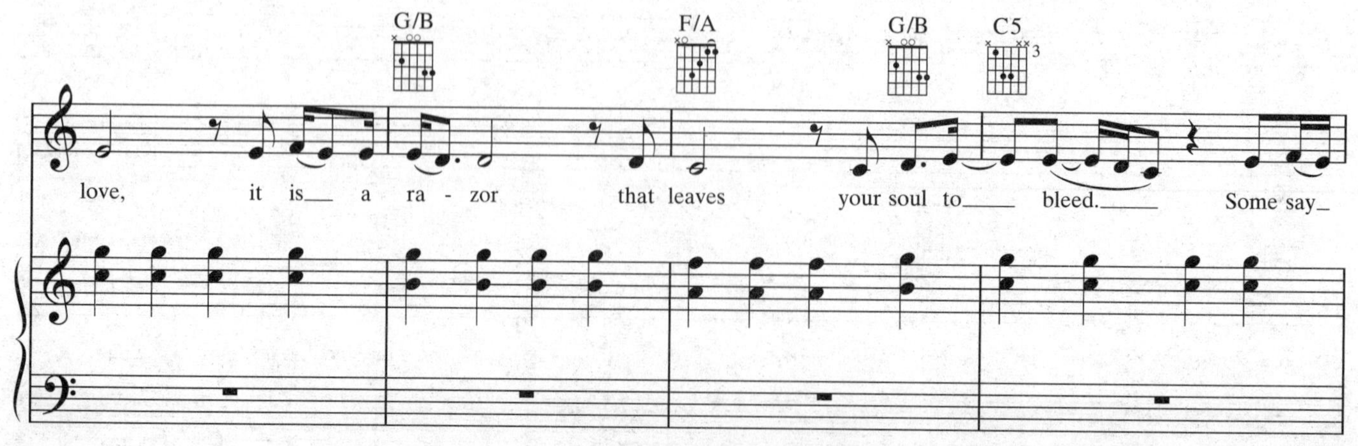

Cmaj7/B
Am7
F/A
love, it is a hun - ger, an end - less, ach - ing
mp
F/G
G7
C5
G/B
need. I say love, it is a flow - er and
poco rit.
p a tempo
F/A
G/B
C(9)
you its on - ly seed. 2. It's the
mp
cresc.
Verse 2:
G(9)
F(9)
G
C(9)
heart a-fraid of break-ing that nev-er learns to dance. It's the
mf

G(9)
F(9)
G
C(9)
dream a-fraid of wak-ing that nev-er takes the chance. It's the
Em7/B
Am
Am/G
F(9)
G(9)
one who won't be tak-en who can-not seem to give, and the
dim.
poco rit.
C(9)
G(9)
F(9)
G
C
soul a-fraid of dy-ing that nev-er learns to live.
mp
a tempo
cresc.
8vb
Verse 3:
G
F
G
3. When the night has been too lone-ly and the road has been too
f
(8vb)

C
G
F
G
long, and you think that love is on - ly for the luck - y and the
(8vb)
C
Em7
Am
F(9)
strong, just re - mem - ber in the win - ter, far be - neath the bit - ter
decresc.
mp
(8vb)
G(9)
C(9)
G(9)
F(9)
G(9)
snows, lies the seed that with the sun's love in the spring be - comes the
poco rit.
p a tempo
C(9)
rose.
rit.

SOUTHERN NIGHTS

Words and Music by
ALLEN TOUSSAINT

Am7
men - tion the trees, whis - tling tunes that you know and love so.
just be - yond the eye. It goes run - ning through your soul like the sto -
C7
F
D7
South - ern nights, just as good e - ven when
- ries told of old. Old man, he and his dog that walked the
G7
Bbmaj7
closed your eyes. I a - pol - o - gize
old land, ev - 'ry flow - er touched
Am7
to an - y - one who can tru - ly say that he has
his cold hand. As he slow - ly walked by, weep - ing

C7
1,2
Guitar Tacet
found a bet - ter way.
wil - lows would cry for joy.
F
D7
G7
Feel so good, feel so good it's fright - 'ning. Wish I could
B♭maj7
stop this world from fight - ing. La da da da da da la da da da da da

Am7
C7
da da da da da
da da da
da da da.
F
D7
Mys - ter - ies
like this and man - y oth - ers
G7
Bbmaj7
in the trees
blow in the night
C7
Guitar Tacet
D.S. (vocal ad lib) and Fade
in the south - ern skies.

STAIRWAY TO HEAVEN

Words and Music by
JIMMY PAGE and ROBERT PLANT

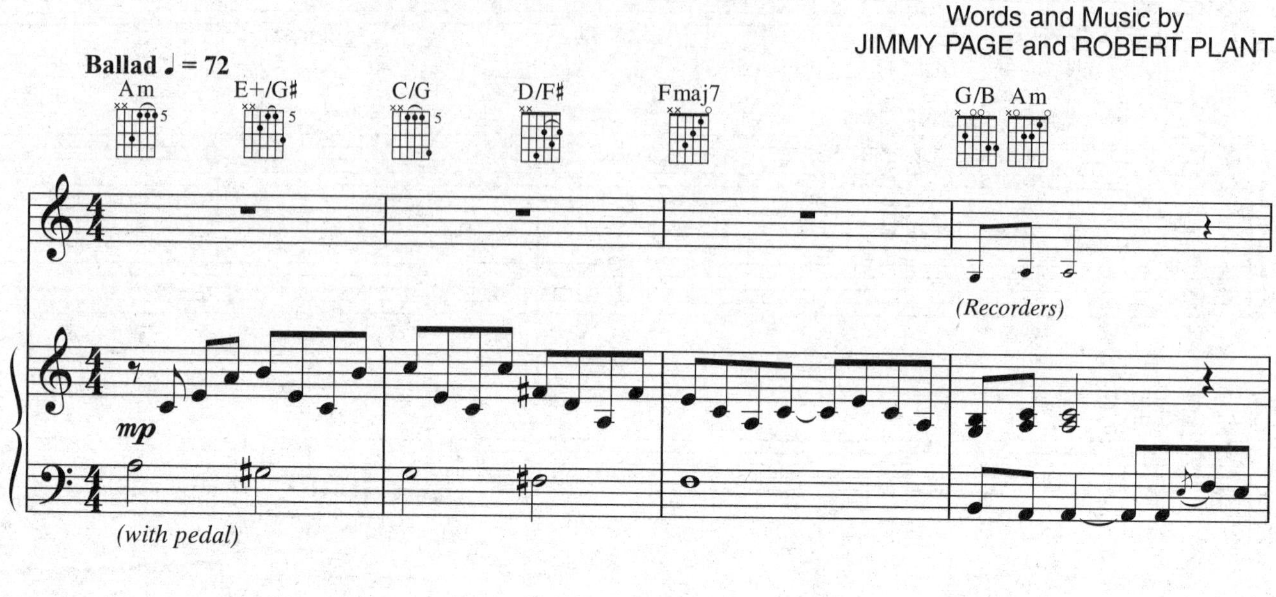

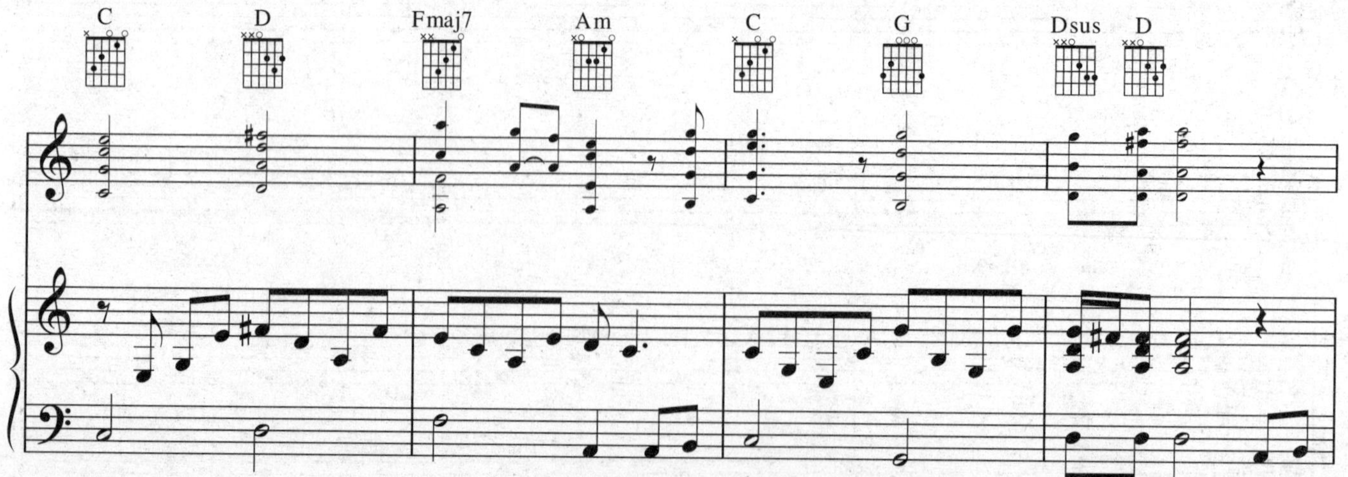

Stairway to Heaven - 12 - 1

C
D
Fmaj7
Am
C
D
Fmaj7
1. There's a
Verse 1:
Am
E+/G♯
C/G
D/F♯
Fmaj7
la - dy who's sure all that glit - ters is gold,_ and she's buy - ing_ a stair-way to
G/B Am
Am
E+/G♯
C/G
D/F♯
heav - en. When she gets there, she knows_ if the stores are all closed,_ with a
Fmaj7
G/B Am
C
D
word she_ can get what she came_ for. Ooo,

Fmaj7
Am
C
G
Dsus
D
ooo, ooo, and she's buy - ing a stair - way to heav - en. There's a
C
D
Fmaj7
Am
C
D
sign on the wall, but she wants to be sure, 'cause you know some - times words have two
Fmaj7
Am
E+/G♯
C/G
D/F♯
mean - ings. In a tree by the brook, there's a song - bird who sings, some - times
Fmaj7
G/B
Am
Am
E+/G♯
all of our thoughts are mis - giv - en.

C/G
D/F♯
Fmaj7
G/B
Am
G/B
Slightly faster
Am7
Dsus
D
Am7
Em/D
Ooo, it makes me won - der.
D
C/D
D
Am7
Dsus
D
Ooo, makes me won - der.
Am7
Em/D
D
C/D
D
2. There's a

Verses 2 & 3:
C
G/B
Am
C
G/B
Fmaj7
feel - ing I get when I look to the west, and my spir - it is cry - ing for leav -
whis - pered that soon if we all call the tune, then the pip - er will lead us to rea -
Am
C
G/B
Am
3
ing. In my thoughts I have seen rings of smoke through the trees, and the
son. And a new day will dawn, for those who stand long, and the
C
G/B
Fmaj7
Am
C
G/B
voic - es of those who stand look - ing.
for - ests will ech - o with laugh - ter.
Am7
Dsus
D
Am7
Em/D
Ooh, it makes me won - der.

D
C/D
D
Am7
Dsus
D
Ooo, it real-ly makes me won-der.
Am7
Em/D
1.
D
C/D
D
2.
D
C/D
D
3. And it's
accel.
Faster (♩ = 88)
Verses 4 & 5:
C
G/B
Am
C
G/B
Fmaj7
4. If there's a bus-tle in your hedge-row, don't be a-larmed now, it's just a spring clean for the May
5. Your head is hum-ming and it won't go, in case you don't know, the pip-er's call-ing you to join
mf
Am
C
G/B
Am
Queen. Yes, there are two paths you can go by, but in the long run,
him. Dear la-dy, can you hear the wind blow, and did you know,

C
G/B
Fmaj7
Am
C
G/B
there's still time to change the road you're on.
your stair-way lies on the whis - p'rin' wind.
1.
Am7
Dsus
D
Am7
Em/D
And it makes me won - der,
D
C/D
D
Am7
Dsus
D
ahh.
Am7
Em/D
D
C/D
D
2.
D

D2
D
Dsus
C(9)
C(9)♯11
G/B
f
Guitar Solo:
Am
C/G
F
Fmaj7

Am
C/G
F
Fmaj7
Am
C/G
F
Fmaj7
Am
C/G
F
Fmaj7
Am
C/G
Fmaj7
Am
C/G

Fmaj7
Am
C/G
Fmaj7
Am
C/G
Fmaj7
Am
G
F
G
Am
G
And as we wind_ on down the road,__
our shad - ows tall - er than our soul.__
F
G
Am
G
F
G
There walks a la - dy we all know,____

Am
G
F
G
Am
G
who shines white light and wants to show_ how ev - 'ry - thing_ still turns to
F
G
Am
G
F
G
gold._____ And if you lis - ten ver - y hard,_____
Am
G
F
G
Am
G
Fmaj7
the tune will come to you_ at last._____ When all are one_ and one is all,_

Am
G
Fmaj7
to be a rock and not to roll.
Am
C/G
Fmaj7
Am
C/G
Fmaj7
Am
C/G
Fmaj7
Am
C/G
rit.
Fmaj7
N.C.
And she's buy - ing a stair - way to heav - en.
mf

SUNDOWN

Words and Music by
GORDON LIGHTFOOT

* Guitarists: Please note that the chord diagrams are in the key of E but the piano accompaniment is in the key of F. In order for the guitar to sound in the same key as the piano, use a capo on the 1st fret. You also may adjust the capo to play in any key that fits your own individual vocal range.

D E5
E♭ F

find you bin creep-in' round_ my back stairs._ Sun - down, you
find you bin creep-in' round_ my back stairs._ Some - times I

A D E5
B♭ E♭ F

bet-ter take care_ if I find you bin creep-in' round_ my back stairs._
think it's a sin_ when I feel like I'm win-nin' when I'm los-in' a - gain._

E5
F

She's bin look-in' like a queen in a sail-or's dream, and she
I can see her look-in' fast in her fad-ed jeans; she's a

B7sus4 E5
C7sus4 F

don't al-ways say_ what she real-ly means._ Some - times I
hard lov-in' wom-an, got me feel-in' mean._ Some - times I

A
B♭
D
E♭
think it's a shame — when I get feel - in' bet - ter when I'm
think it's a shame — when I get feel - in' bet - ter when I'm
E5
F
A
B♭
feel - in' no pain. — Some - times I think it's a shame — when I
feel - in' no pain. — Sun - down, you bet - ter take care — if I
D
E♭
To Coda
E5
F
get feel - in' bet - ter when I'm feel - in' no pain. —
find you bin creep - in' round
D. S. al Coda
I can

Coda

E5 F | A B♭

my back stairs._ Sun - down, you bet-ter take care_ if I

D E♭ | E5 F

find you bin creep-in' round_ my back stairs._ Some-times I

A B♭ | D E♭ | E5 F

think it's a sin_ when I feel like I'm win-nin' when I'm los-in' a - gain._

A B♭ | D E♭ | E5 F

TAKE MY BREATH AWAY

(Love Theme from *Top Gun*)

Words by
TOM WHITLOCK

Music by
GIORGIO MORODER

G
D/F♯
Em7
on this end-less o-cean, fi - n'lly lov-ers know no shame.
Nev-er hes-i-tat-ing to be-come the fat-ed ones.
D/F♯
Am
G
Turn-ing and re-turn-ing to some se-cret place in-side,
D/F♯
G
watch-ing in slow mo-tion as
D/F♯
C(9)/E
D/F♯
you turn a-round and say, my love, "Take my breath a-

Chorus:
G
D/F♯
C(9)/E
way.
D/F♯
G
D/F♯
Take my breath a - way."
1.
2.
C(9)/E
D/F♯
D/F♯
Bridge:
Am
D
C(9)
Through the ho - ur - glass I saw you. In time, you slipped a - way.

G
Am
D
When the mir - ror crashed, I called you and turned
C(9)
G
A(9)
to hear you say, "If on - ly for to - day,
D
N.C.
I am un - a - fraid." Take my breath a -
B♭
F/A
E♭(9)/G
F
Repeat ad lib. and fade
way. Take my breath a -

TAKE ME HOME, COUNTRY ROADS

Words and Music by
JOHN DENVER, BILL DANOFF
and TAFFY NIVERT

E
D
trees, young - er than the moun - tains, grow - in' like a breeze.
sky, mist - y taste of moon - shine, tear - drop in my eye.
A
Chorus:
E
Coun - try roads, take me home
F♯m
D
to the place I be - long.
A
E
West Vir - gin - ia, moun - tain ma - ma,

D
A
take me home,
country roads.
1.
2.
Bridge:
F♯m
E
I hear her voice in the morn-
A
D
A
in' hour; she calls me. The ra-di-o re-minds me of my
E
F♯m
G
home far a-way. And driv-in' down the road, I get a

D
A
E
feel - in' that I should have been home yes - ter - day, yes - ter - day.
E7
Chorus:
A
Coun - try roads, take me home
E
F♯m
to the place I be - long.
D
A
West Vir - gin - ia, moun - tain ma -

E
D
ma, take me home, coun - try roads.
A
1.
2.
E
Coun - try roads, Take me home,
A
E
coun - try roads. Take me home,
A
D/E
A
coun - try roads.

THIS MASQUERADE

Words and Music by
LEON RUSSELL

Fm7
Fm(maj7)
Fm7
Are we real - ly hap - py here_ with this lone - ly game we play,_
B♭13
Fm9
D♭7
looking for words_ to say?_
Gm11
C7(♭9 ♯5)
Fm7
Search - ing but not find -
Fm(maj7)
Fm7
B♭9
ing un - der - stand - ing an - y - way,_ we're

D♭13(♯11)
C7
Fm7
lost in a mas, masquer-ade.
Em7
A13
E♭m9
A♭13(♭9)
Both a-fraid to say we're just too far
D♭maj9
B♭7(♭9 ♯5)
E♭m9
a-way from be-ing close to-geth-
A♭13(♭9)
D♭maj7
er from the start.
We

Dm7
G13
Cmaj9
tried to talk it o - ver, but the words got in the way.
Gm11
G13
G7(♯5)
We're lost in - side this lone -
C9sus
G♭13
Fm7
ly game we play.
Thoughts of leav - ing dis -
Fm(maj7)
Fm7
B♭9
ap - pear ev - 'ry time I see your eyes,

Fm7 D♭9 Gm11

no mat-ter how hard I try

C7(♯9 ♯5) Fm7 Fm(maj7)

to un-der-stand the rea - sons that we

Fm7 B♭9 D♭13 C7(♯9 ♯5)

car-ry on this way. We're lost in a mas - quer-ade.

Repeat ad lib. and fade

Fm7 B♭13 Fm7 B♭13

UP WHERE WE BELONG

Words by
WILL JENNINGS

Music by
JACK NITZSCHE and
BUFFY SAINTE-MARIE

D
D7/F♯
D
D7/F♯
Em7
real, I keep it a - live.
The road is
A
D
D/F♯
G
G/B
long.
There are moun - tains in our way, but we
C
D/C
A
G/A
A
Chorus:
D
D/F♯
climb a step ev - 'ry day.
Love lift us up where we be - long,
cresc.
f
G
Bm
Em
D/F♯
C
G
A
where the ea - gles cry on a moun - tain high.

D
D/F♯
Bm
Em
D/F♯
Love lift us up where we be - long,
far from the world we know;
up where the
1.
F♯/A♯
Bm
Gm
D
G/D
Gm/D
clear winds blow.
decresc.
mp
2.
Bridge:
G/A
A
F
C/E
E♭
B♭/D
clear winds blow.
Time goes by,
no time to cry,
decresc.
D♭
A♭/C
B♭
Fm7/B♭
life's you and I,
a - live
to - day.
cresc. poco a poco

Chorus:

E♭ E♭/G A♭ Cm Fm E♭/G

Love lift us up where we be - long, where the ea - gles cry on a

D♭ A♭ B♭ E♭ E♭/G A♭ Cm

moun - tain high. Love lift us up where we be - long, far from the

Repeat ad lib. and fade

Fm E♭/G G/B Cm A♭m

world we know; up where the clear winds blow.

Verse 2:
Some hang on to "used-to-be,"
Live their lives looking behind.
All we have is here and now;
All our life, out there to find.
The road is long.
There are mountains in our way,
But we climb a step every day.
(To Chorus:)

WAKE ME UP BEFORE YOU GO-GO

Words and Music by
GEORGE MICHAEL

Brightly ♩ = 168

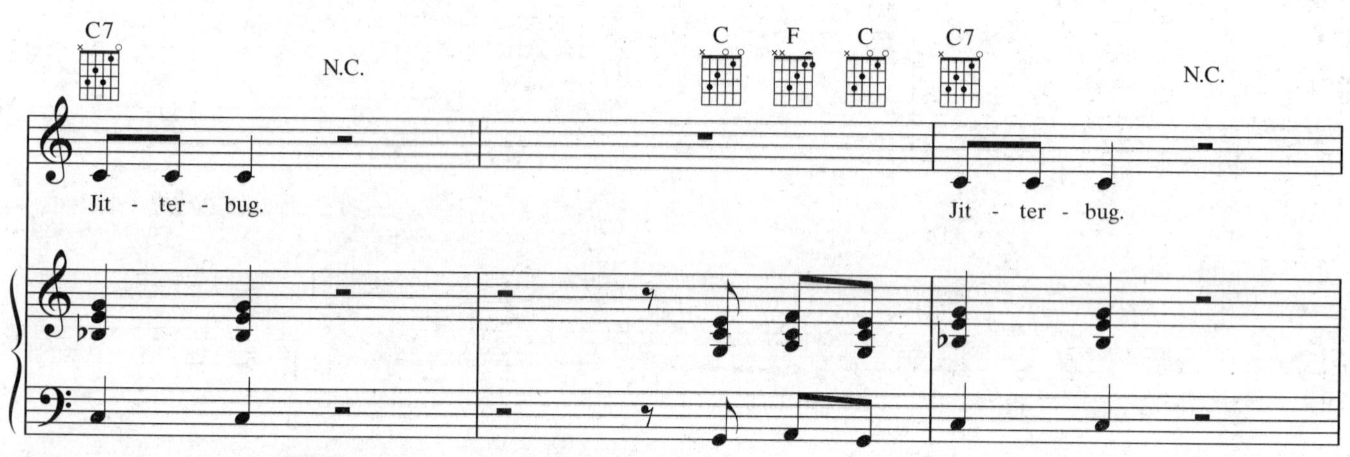

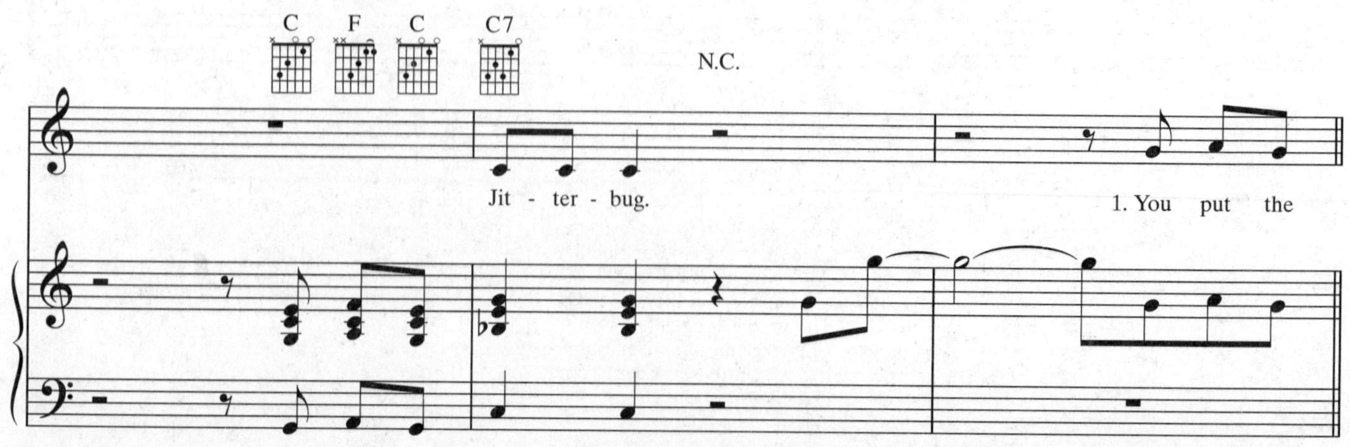

Verses 1 & 2:
C
Dm
boom boom in - to my heart.
(2.) grey skies out - ta my way.
You send my soul sky high when your
You make the sun shine bright-er than
lov - in' starts. A jit - ter - bug in - to my brain, it goes a -
Do - ris Day. You turn a bright spark in - to a flame. My
bang bang bang till my feet do the same. If some-thin's bug - gin' you, if
beats per min - ute nev - er been the same. 'Cause you're my la - dy;
Em
F
G/A
some - thin' ain't right, my best friend told me what you did last night.
I'm your fool. It makes me cra - zy when you act so cruel.

Dm
Em
F
Left me sleep - in' in my bed;
Come on, ba - by, let's not fight.
I was dream - in', but I
We'll go danc - ing;
G
C/G
G
N.C.
Chorus:
C
should have been with you in - stead.
ev - 'ry - thing - 'll be all right.
Wake me up be-fore you go -
Dm
C
go; don't leave me hang - in' on like a yo - yo.
Wake me up
Dm
be - fore you go - go; I don't wan - na miss it when you hit that high.

C
Wake me up before you go - go, 'cause I'm not plan-
Dm
C
nin' on go - in' so - lo. Wake me up before you go-
To Coda
C7
Dm
C9
F/C
go; take me danc - in' to - night.
C7
C9
F/C
I wan - na hit that high.

1.
C7
Yeah, yeah.
2. You put the
2.
C7
Yeah, yeah, yeah.
Verse 3:
C
3. Jit - ter - bug.
(Inst. solo behind vocal…
Dm
C
3
Jit - ter - bug.
Dm
C
…end solo)
Dm
Em
F
Em
G/A
3
Cud - dle up, ba - by, move in tight.
We'll go danc - ing to - mor - row night.
It's

Dm
Em
F
F/G
cold out there, but it's warm in bed. They can dance; we'll stay home in - stead.
C
Dm
C
D.S. 𝄋 al Coda
Dm
C9
Dm
C
Jit - ter-bug.
Wake me up
Coda
Dm
C7
Dm
C
Chorus:
take me danc - in' to - night. Wake me up be - fore you go -

Dm
C
go; don't leave me hang - in' on like a yo - yo. Wake me up
Dm
C
before you go - go; I don't wan-na miss it when you hit that high. Wake me up
Dm
C
before you go - go, 'cause I'm not plan - nin' on go - in' so - lo. Wake me up
Repeat ad lib. and fade
Dm
C7
Dm
C
be - fore you go - go; take me danc - in' to - night. Wake me up

WILD HORSES

Words and Music by
MICK JAGGER and KEITH RICHARDS

Bm
G
Gsus
G
is eas - y to do.
a dull aching pain.
a sin and a lie.
Am
G
C
D
The things you want - ed,
Now you de - cid - ed
I have my free - dom,
G
Gsus
G
D
C
I bought them for you.
to show me the same.
but I don't have much time.
Bm
G
Gsus
G
Grace - less la - dy,
No sweep-ing ex - its
Faith has been bro - ken,

Bm
G
Gsus
G
you know who I am.
or off-stage lines
tears must be cried.
Am
G
C
D
You know I can't let you
could make me feel bit - ter
Let's do some liv - ing
G
Gsus
G
D
slide through my hands.
or treat you un - kind.
af - ter we die.
Chorus:
Am
C
D
D7
G
F
Wild horses couldn't drag me a -

To Coda
C
Bm
Am
C
D
D7
way.
Wild,
wild
hors - es
1.
G
F
C
2.
G
F
could - n't drag
me
a -
way.
could - n't drag
me
a -
C
F(9)
C
way.
(Gtr. solo…
F(9)
C
D
G
Gsus
G
…end solo)

3.
G
F
C
we'll ride them some - day.
Solo:
Bm
G
Gsus
G
Bm
G
Gsus
G
(Lead Gtr.)
p
D.S. 𝄋 al Coda
Am
G
C
D
G
Gsus
G
D
G/D
(end Gtr.)
mf
Coda
G
F
C
G
we'll ride them some - day.

WE ARE THE WORLD

Written and Composed by
MICHAEL JACKSON and LIONEL RICHIE

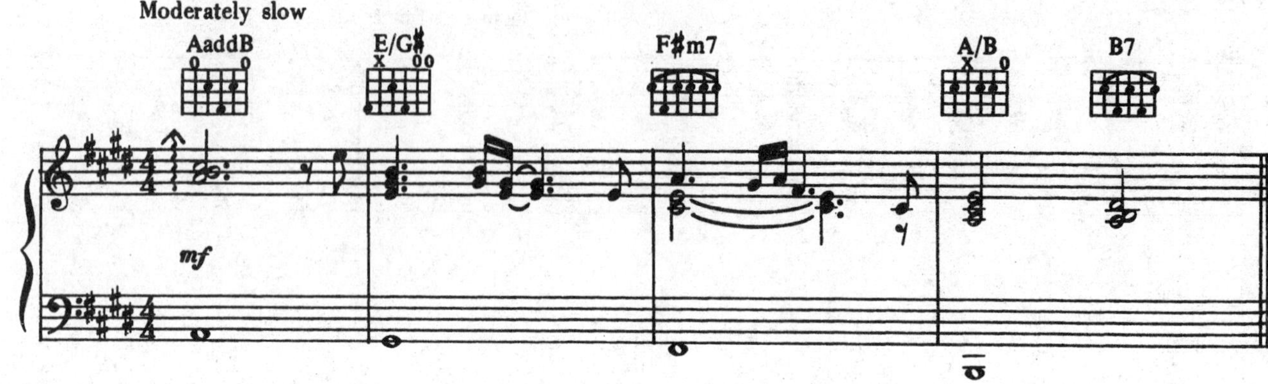

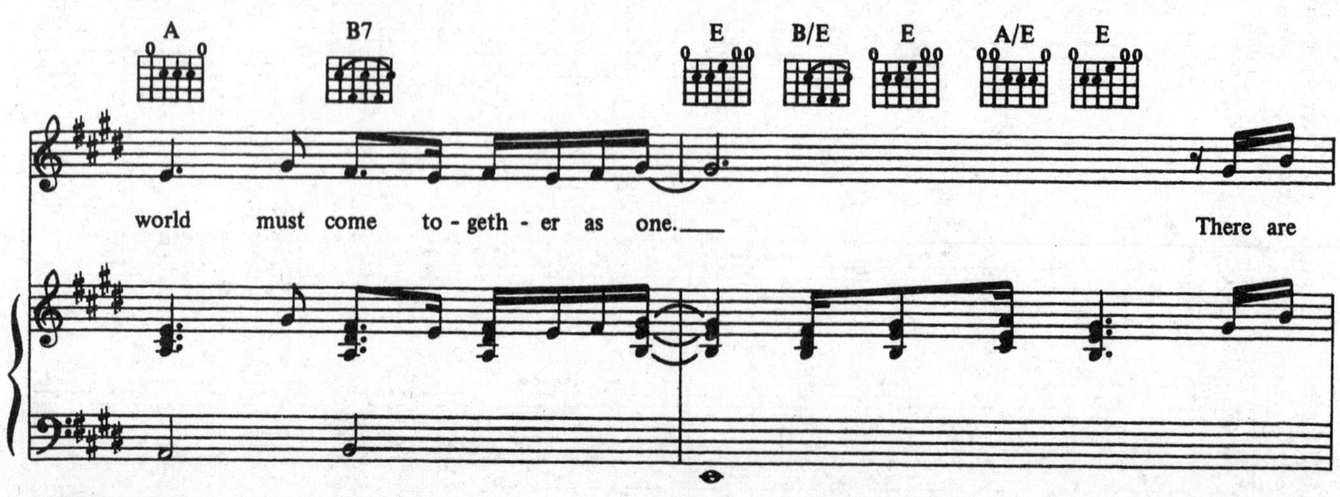

C#m
4fr.
G#m
4fr.
F#m7
F#m7/A
peo-ple dy - ing ___ and it's time to lend a hand ___ to life, the great-est gift ___ of all. ___
Bsus4
2 fr.
B
E
A/E
B/E
E
We can't go on ___ pre-tend-ing day ___ by day ___ that some-
Send them your heart ___ so they'll know that some - one cares ___ and their
A
B7
E
A/E
E
C#m
4fr.
3
one, some-where will soon make a change. We are all a part ___ of ___ God's
lives will be strong-er and free. As God has shown ___ us ___ by
G#m
4fr.
F#m7
F#m7/A
great big fam - i - ly ___ and the truth, you know, love is all we need. ___
turn - ing stone ___ to bread, ___ so we all must lend a help - ing hand. ___

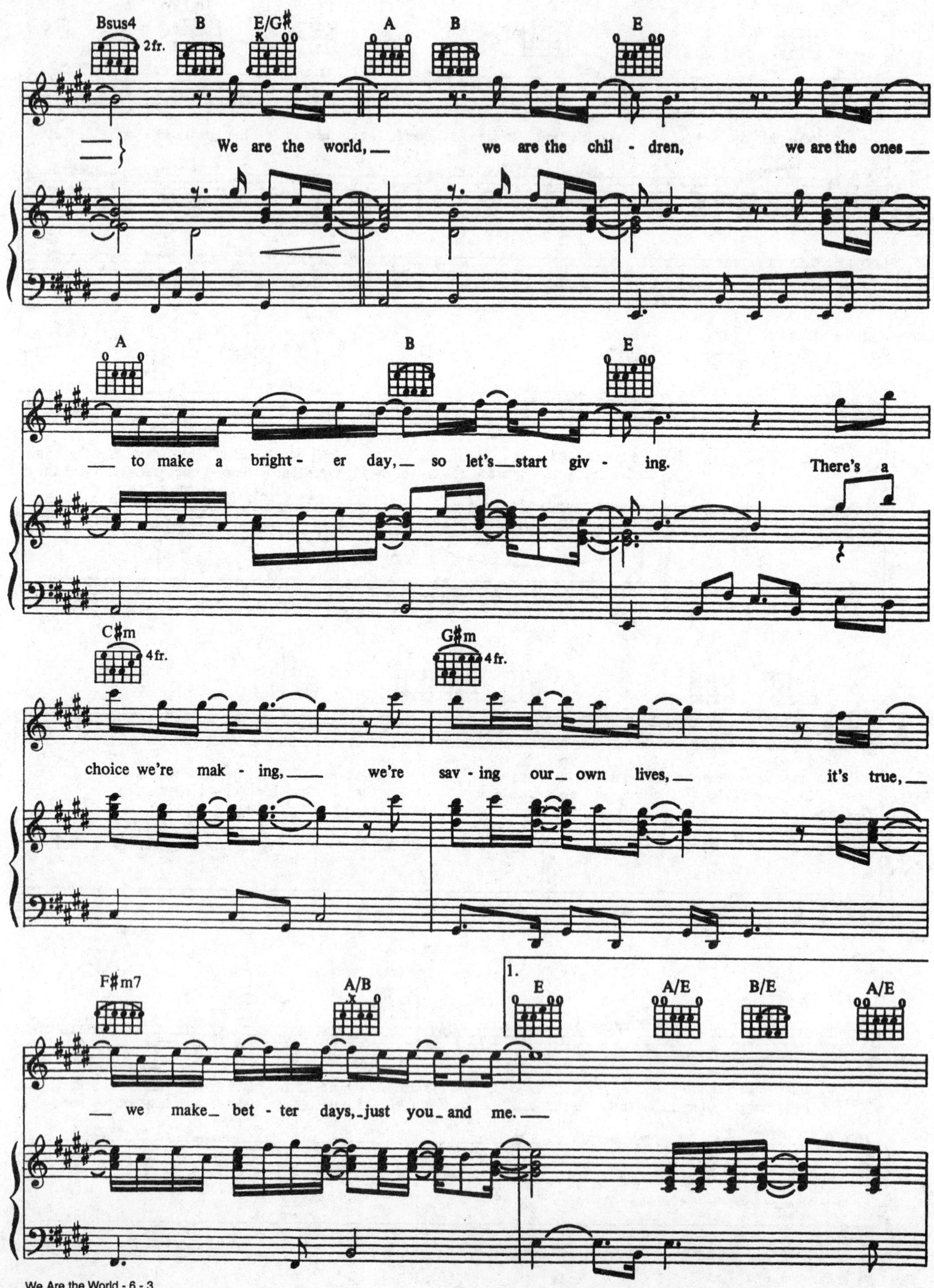
Bsus4
2fr.
B
E/G♯
A
B
E
We are the world, we are the chil - dren, we are the ones
A
B
E
to make a bright - er day, so let's start giv - ing. There's a
C♯m
4fr.
G♯m
4fr.
choice we're mak - ing, we're sav - ing our own lives, it's true,
F♯m7
A/B
1.
E
A/E
B/E
A/E
we make bet - ter days, just you and me.

E
A/E
B/E
A/E
2.
E
When you're
C
D
E
A/E
E
down and out, there seems no hope at all,
but if you
f
C
D
E
just be - lieve, there's no way we can fall.
Let us
C♯m
4fr.
G♯m
4fr.
F♯m7
F♯m7/A
re - al - ize
that a change will on - ly come when we
stand to-geth - er as

Bsus4
2 fr.
B
A
B
E
one. We are the world, we are the chil - dren, we are the ones
A
B
E
to make a bright- er day, so let's start giv - ing. There's a
C#m
4 fr.
G#m
4 fr.
choice we're mak - ing, we're sav - ing our own lives, it's true;
F#m7
A/B
1.
E
E/G#
we make bet - ter days, just you and me. We are the world,

2.
Repeat and fade
E
F
F
C
F
We are the world, we are the chil - dren; we are the ones
ff
Bb
C
F
to make a bright - er day, so let's start giv - ing.
There's a
Dm
Am
choice we're mak - ing, we're sav - ing our own lives, it's true,
Gm7
3 fr.
Bb/C
F
Eb/G
F/A
we make bet - ter days, just you and me.
We are the world,

THE WIND BENEATH MY WINGS

Words and Music by
LARRY HENLEY and JEFF SILBAR

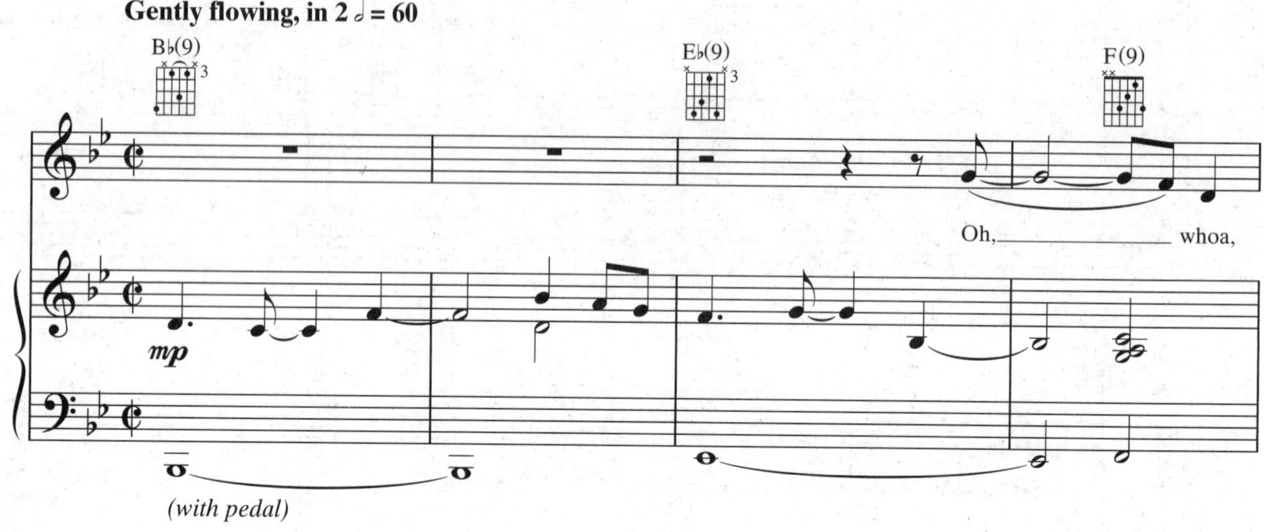

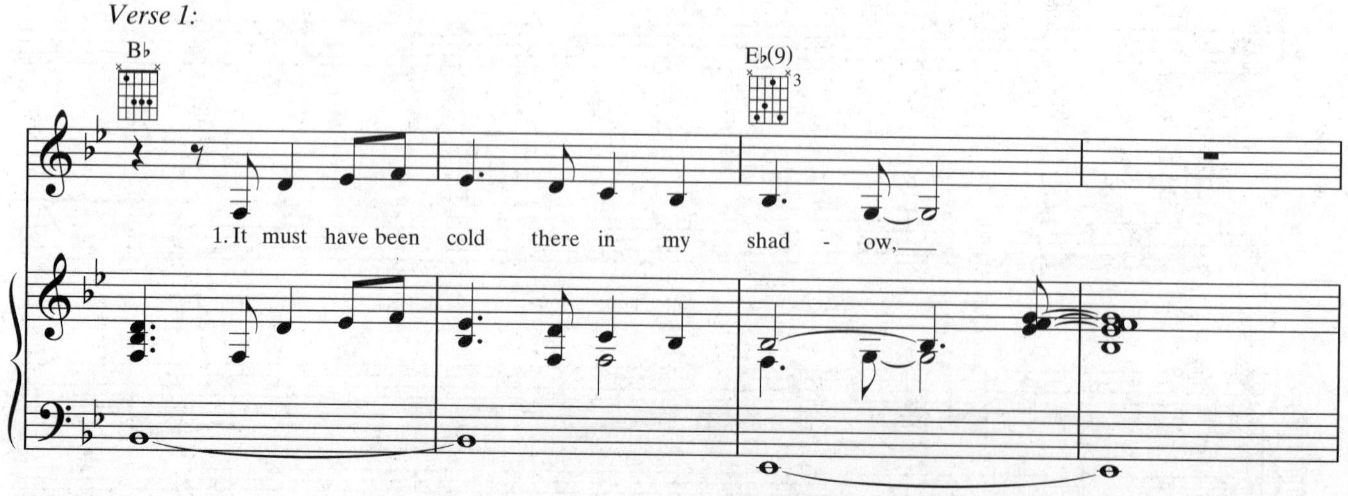

Bb
Eb(9)
to nev-er have sun - light on your face.
Cm7
Fsus
F
You were con - tent to let me shine, that's your way,
Cm7
Fsus
F
you al-ways walked a step be - hind.
Verses 2 & 3:
Bb
Eb(9)
2. So, I was the one with all the glo - ry,
3. It might have ap-peared to go un - no - ticed,

B♭
E♭(9)
Gm7
while you__ were the one with all__ the strength.
but I've__ got it all here in__ my heart.
Cm7
B♭/C
Fsus
F
A beau - ti - ful face with - out__ a name__ for so long,__
I want you to know I know__ the truth,__ of course I know__ it,
Cm7
B♭/C
Fsus
F
D/F♯
a beau - ti - ful smile to hide__ the pain.
I__ would be noth - ing with - out you.
Chorus:
Gm7
F/E♭
E♭
B♭
F/A
Did you ev - er know__ that
Did I ev - er tell__ you
you're__ my he - ro,

Gm7
F/E♭
E♭
B♭
F/A
D/F♯
1. and ev - 'ry - thing I would like to be?
2.3. and ev - 'ry - thing I wish I could be?
3
Gm7
F/E♭
E♭
B♭
F/A
Gm7
I can fly high - er than an ea - gle,
To Coda
1.
Cm7
Fsus
F
B♭(9)
for you are the wind be-neath my wings.
E♭(9)
2.
D.S. al Coda
B♭
E♭/B♭
B♭
F/A
wings.

Coda
E♭/B♭
B♭
Cm7
wings.
'Cause you are the
Fsus
F
B♭(9)
wind beneath my wings, oh, the
E♭(9)
F7sus
B♭
wind be-neath my wings. You, you, you are the
E♭/B♭
B♭
wind be-neath my wings. Fly,

E♭/B♭
B♭
B♭/D
fly, fly a - way, you let
E♭(9)
F/A
B♭
me fly so high. Oh, you, you, you, the
E♭/B♭
B♭
B♭/D
wind be - neath my wings. Oh, you, you, the
E♭(9)
F/A
B♭
wind be - neath my wings. Fly,

E♭/B♭
B♭
B♭/D
fly, so high a - gainst the sky, so high

E♭(9)
F9sus
F/A
B♭
I al - most touch the sky. Thank you, thank

E♭/B♭
B♭sus
B♭(9)
you, thank God for you, the wind be - neath my wings.

WISH YOU WERE HERE

Words and Music by
ROGER WATERS and DAVID GILMOUR

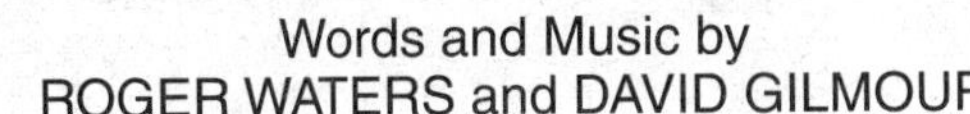

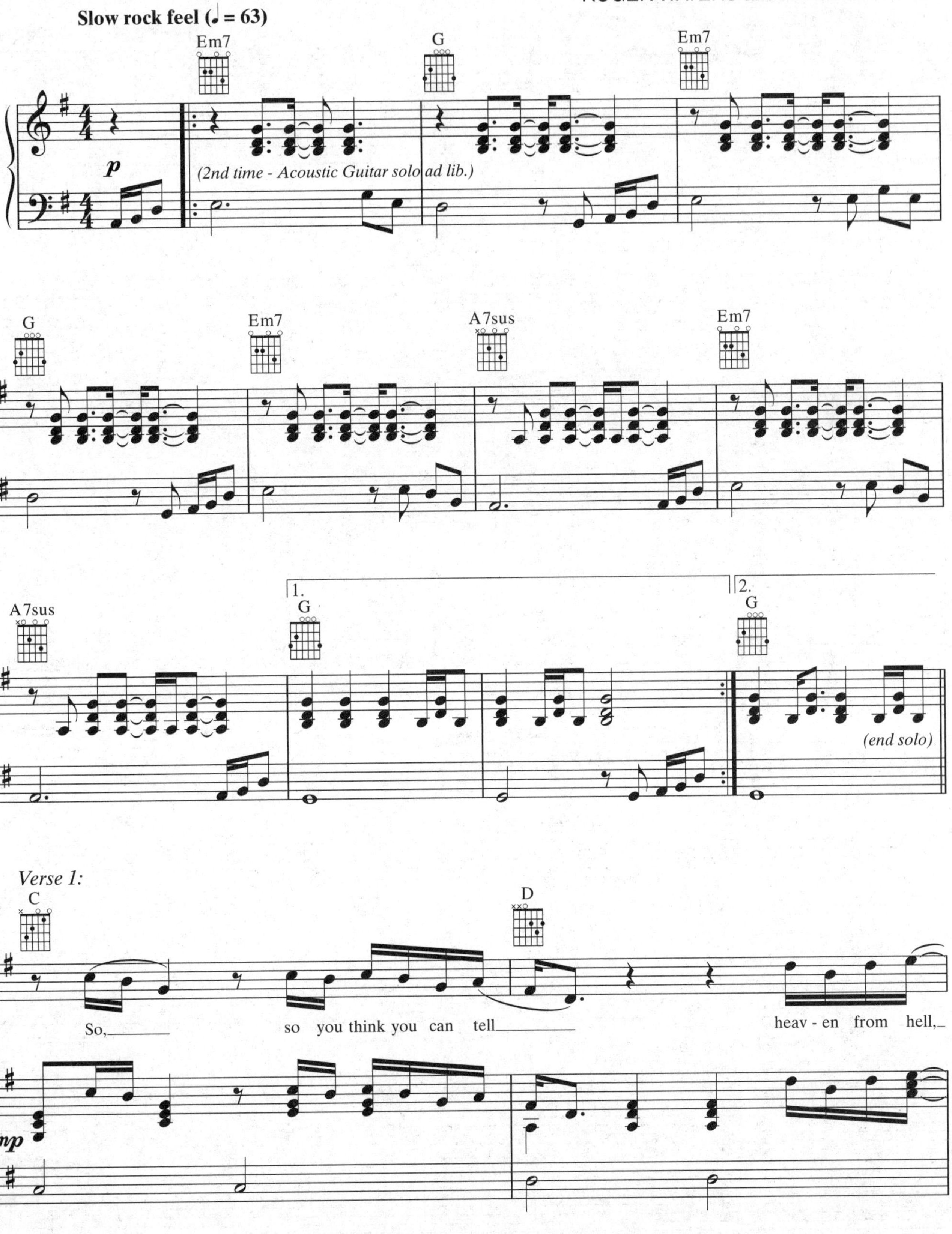

Slow rock feel (♩ = 63)
Em7
G
Em7
p
(2nd time - Acoustic Guitar solo ad lib.)
G
Em7
A7sus
Em7
A7sus
1.
G
2.
G
(end solo)
Verse 1:
C
D
So,
so you think you can tell
heav - en from hell,
mp

Am
G
blue skys from pain.
Can you tell a green field
D/F♯
C
from a cold steel rail?
A smile from a veil?
Am
G
Do you think you can tell?
Did they get you to trade
mf
Verse 2:
C
D
your he - roes for ghosts?
Hot ash - es for trees?

Am
G
Hot air for a cool breeze? Cold com-fort for change?
D/F♯
C
And did you ex-change a walk-on part in the war
Am
G
Em7
for a lead role in a cage?
Dobro solo ad lib.
dim.
mp
G
Em7
G
Em7

A7sus
Em7
A7sus
G
cresc.
Chorus:
C
D
How I wish, how I wish you were here. We're just
mf
Am
G
two lost souls swim-ming in a fish bowl, year af - ter year,
D
C
run-ning o - ver the same old ground. What have we found? The same old

Am G

fears.____ Wish you____ were here.____

Ending:

Em G Em

(2nd time - Dobro doubled by scat vocal cont.)

mp

G Em A

Em A G

Repeat and fade

(1st time - Dobro doubled by scat vocal)

WOODEN SHIPS

Words and Music by
PAUL KANTNER, DAVID CROSBY
and STEPHEN STILLS

Verse 1:

Em7 10 | Am9 10 | F/A 10

smile at___ me, I will un - der - stand, 'cause that___ is some-thing

Em7 10 | Am9 10 | F/A 10

ev - 'ry - bod - y ev - 'ry-where does in___ the same_______ lan -

Em7 10 | Am9 10 | F/A 10

guage.___ *(Inst. solo ad lib....*

Em7 10 | Am9 10 | F/A 10

Second Voice:

...end solo) 2. I can

Verse 2:
Em7
10
Am9
10
F/A
10
see by your coat, my friend, you're from the oth - er side. There's just
Em7
Am9
F/A
Em7
one thing I got to know, can you tell me, please: Who won?
Am9
F/A
Em7
Am
F/A
Verse 3:
Em7
Am9
F/A
First voice:
Second Voice:
3. Say, can I have some of your pur-ple ber-ries? Yes, I've been eat-ing them for six

Em7
Am9
F/A
First voice:
or sev - en weeks now; have-n't got sick once. Prob - 'bly keep us both
Em7
Am9
F/A
D
A
G
a - live.
mf
Chorus 1:
Em
A
D2
Wood-en ships on the wa - ter, ver - y free, and eas - y.
Em
A
D2
Eas - y, you know, the way it's sup - posed to be.

Em
A
D2
Sil - ver
peo - ple
on the shore - line,
let
us
be.
Talk - in' 'bout
Double-time feel
Cmaj7
Em9
ver - y
free
and
eas - y.
(Inst. solo ad lib. behind vocal...
Cmaj7
Em9
Cmaj7
Em9

Cmaj7
D2
…end solo)
Tempo I
Chorus 2 & 3:
Em
A
D2
2. Hor - ror grips us as___ we___ watch you___ die.___
3. (Inst. solo ad lib.…
Em
A
D2
All we can_ do is ech - o your an - guished_ cries.___
Em
A
D2
Stare as all hu-man feel - ings__ die.____ We are

Cmaj7
Em9
leav - ing; you don't need us.
(Inst. solo ad lib. behind vocal 1st time...
Cmaj7
Em9
Cmaj7
Em9
Cmaj7
1.
D2
...solo cont. in Chorus 3)

2.
Chorus 4:
D2
Em
…end solo)
4. Go, take a sis - ter, then,
A
D2
Em
by the hand, lead her a - way from this
A
D2
Em
for - eign land, far a - way, where we might
A
D2
Cmaj7
laugh a - gain. We are leav - ing; you don't

Em9
Cmaj7
need
need us.
(Inst. solo ad lib. behind vocal…
Em9
Cmaj7
us.
Em9
Cmaj7
(Inst. solo ad lib. cont.…
1.
Em9
Cmaj7

2.
Cmaj7
Em9
…end solo)
And it's a fair wind,
blow-in' warm out of the south o - ver my shoul - der;
guess I'll set a course and go.
rit.
Ped.

YOU LIGHT UP MY LIFE

Words and Music by
JOE BROOKS

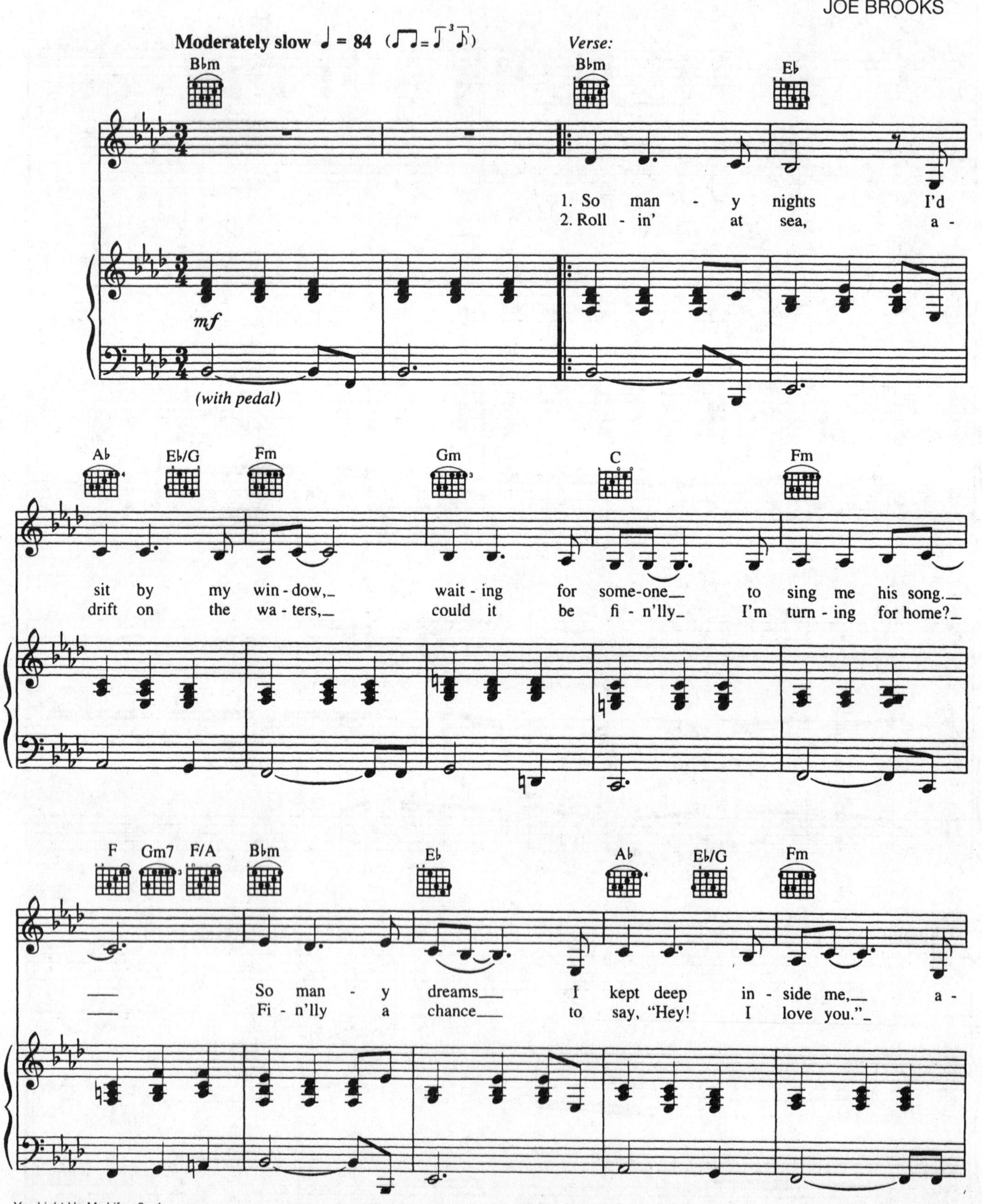

G
B♭
Cm7
B♭/D
lone in the dark, now you've come a - long.
Nev - er a - gain to be all a - lone.
And
E♭
E♭maj7
E♭7
C7
you light up my life. You give me hope
Fm
Fm7
B♭7
To Coda
to car - ry on. You light up my days and fill my
1.
E♭
B♭/D
Cm7
Fm
Fm7
B♭
nights with song.

D.S. 𝄋 al Coda
2.
Eb
Bb/D
Cm7
Fm
Fm7
Bb
Cm7
Bb/D
nights with song. 'Cause
Coda
G7
G7/B
Cm
F7
Eb/Bb
nights with song. It can't be wrong when
G7/B
Cm7
F9
Eb/Bb
Bb7sus
it feels so right, 'cause you,
Bb7
Ab
Eb
Bb7
Ab(9)
Eb/G
Fm7
Eb
you light up my life.
rit.
a little slower